THE FELLOWSHIP

THE FELLOWSHIP

An Expositional Study of

I JOHN

by
GUY H. KING

CHRISTIAN LITERATURE CRUSADE
Fort Washington, Pennsylvania 19034

CHRISTIAN LITERATURE CRUSADE

Fort Washington, Pennsylvania 19034

*This edition published under
special arrangement with*

Marshall, Morgan & Scott, Ltd.
116 Baker Street
London W1M 2BB

ISBN 0-87508-279-3

FOREWORD

WHOSO embarks upon a sincere and serious study of this Epistle lays himself open to much humbling of heart. Yet that same heart will soon—perhaps on account of its very humbling—find itself enraptured with what it here shall find. The Life, the Light, and the Love of the Fellowship will make him bless God that, by His grace, he ever came to belong, and pray God that, by His power, he may ever seek properly to behave.

Many titles for the Epistle have been suggested by its various expositors. For my own part, I have for long felt that its early discussion of " fellowship " is the clue to the whole. I have recently found corroboration in words of Dr. Marvin Vincent of New York, who wrote, " the keynote of fellowship pervades the Epistle." If I have seemed, in places, over-dogmatic in support of my own interpretations, forgive the wrongful spirit—but study the point all the more carefully, in case I am right !

May the Divine Head of the Fellowship deign to use this Study, spite of all its faults and shortcomings, to the blessing of some of its Members.

G. H. K.

CHRIST CHURCH VICARAGE,
BECKENHAM

CONTENTS

A PRAYER OF THE FELLOWSHIP

Master, speak! Thy servant heareth,
  Waiting for Thy gracious word.
Longing for Thy voice that cheereth,
  Master, let it now be heard.
I am listening, Lord, for Thee.
  What hast Thou to say to me?

Master, speak! Though least and lowest,
  Let me not unheard depart;
Master, speak! for, oh, Thou knowest
  All the yearning of my heart,
Knowest all its truest need,
  Speak! and make me blest indeed.

Master, Speak! and make me ready,
  When Thy voice is truly heard,
With obedience glad and steady,
  Still to follow every word.
I am listening, Lord, for Thee,
  Master, speak, oh speak to me.

Speak to me by name, O Master,
  Let me know it is to me,
Speak that I may follow faster,
  With a step more firm and free,
Where the Shepherd leads the flock,
  In the shadow of the Rock.

F. R. HAVERGAL.

I

THE PLEASURE OF THE FELLOWSHIP

I JOHN i. 1–7

1 That which was from the beginning, which we have heard, which we have seen with our eyes, which we have looked upon, and our hands have handled, of the Word of life ;

2 (For the life was manifested, and we have seen *it*, and bear witness, and shew unto you that eternal life, which was with the Father, and was manifested unto us ;)

3 That which we have seen and heard declare we unto you, that ye also may have fellowship with us ; and truly our fellowship *is* with the Father, and with his Son Jesus Christ.

4 And these things write we unto you, that your joy may be full.

5 This then is the message which we have heard of him, and declare unto you, that God is light, and in him is no darkness at all.

6 If we say that we have fellowship with him, and walk in darkness, we lie, and do not the truth :

7 But if we walk in the light, as he is in the light, we have fellowship one with another, and the blood of Jesus Christ his Son cleanseth us from all sin.

" THESE things write we unto you that your joy may be full," says verse 4. There was so much in the conditions and circumstances of the Early Church—persecution, loneliness, atmosphere, martyrdom—which might be supposed to depress those first Christians ; but there were over riding blessings that would minister to " your joy ". Do you recall the circumstances of the occasion when our Lord JESUS spoke of " My joy ", John xv. 11 ? This passage, then, has things to say to its readers, and to us, that will conduce to real joy of heart.

In coming to the expositional study of this Epistle, there is a great deal that is of interest and importance to scholars in the field of New Testament criticism, and the like, that, by the very nature of our own task, need not detain us. The matter of authorship has been widely discussed ; but the old view, that it was written by John the Apostle, has the backing of such distinguished names, of world-wide repute, as Sanday, Armitage Robinson, Salmond, Chase, Ramsay, Westcott, Gore, Moulton, Scroggie, and others. As to date, we are inclined to the opinion that A.D. 95–8 is the period of its composition, making it thus (with the 2nd and 3rd Epistles) the last piece of the New Testament to be written, with the Revelation compiled perhaps thirty years beforehand.   The place where the aged apostle dictated the Letter was probably Ephesus, though it was not specifically addressed to the Church there, being designated as an Epistle General, that is, not meant for any particular place, like the Romans, Corinthians, Galatians, Philippians, Colossians, Thessalonians, but for the Church at large, the Christians in general—for you and me, for instance.   Let us take up the study of it in that light : as a letter addressed personally to us individually.

We turn, then, to our first section, which will underline for us one of the fundamental truths of the Christian religion, that we are saved not for Isolation but for Fellowship : a community whose nature will make for joy and pleasure in all who really belong.   As Psalm xvi. 11 has it, " In Thy presence is fulness of joy : at Thy right hand there are pleasures for evermore ".   Mark that it is—

A FELLOWSHIP OF LIFE (1–2)

There is something so joyous about virile life !   These verses show it to be *A Life which is Eternal*—(*a*) It runs back into the past : " from the beginning " (1).   The Gospel of John (i. 1) says it was " in the beginning ".   The American scholar, Dr. Marvin Vincent, suggests that " in " implies being present before the creation and " from " signifies presence at the time of creation.   Somewhat after the two statements, " the Lamb slain *from* the foundation of the world ", Revelation xiii. 8, and the " Lamb . . . fore-ordained *before* the foundation of the world ", I Peter i. 19–20.   (*b*) It runs on into the future : " that eternal life " (2). Once that life is ours, it never ends for us—" I give unto them eternal life, and they shall never perish ", John x. 28— in the Greek the negative is doubled, and may be rendered, " in no wise ", or " on no account ".   Whatever else is said about this life, it endures—the believer has " eternal " life, John iii. 15, it always has been ; and " everlasting " life, John iii. 16, it always will be.

Further, here is *A Life which is Historical*—it is not something merely theoretical, ethereal :   the Life, for all its pre-existence, did, at a point of time, appear as an event on the stage of human history—" the life which was with the Father . . . was manifested unto us " (2). John was one of the privileged ones, who had " seen " for himself, and so was able to, indeed felt bound to, " shew " the fact to others. A " witness " is a two-sided being—the one side of him *sees*, the other side of him *shows* ; and it is just that dual function that is incumbent upon every true believer—" ye shall be witnesses. . . ." Acts i. 8.

Thus we are led on to see this as *A Life which is Personal*— (a) It is personified in CHRIST. When, in our opening verse, it speaks of " the Word of life ", the capital " W " taking us back to the beginning of the Gospel, it transpires that the Life is not an It, but a He. That runs, almost as a principle, through all the supplies of our spiritual needs. He not merely gives, but is—" I *am* the Bread ", John vi. 35 ; " I *am* the Door ", John x. 7 ; " I *am* the Vine ", John xv. 5 ; " I *am* the resurrection and the life ", John xi. 25. Cf. Micah v. 5, " This Man shall *be* the peace ". Well now, this Life that was the Person, was heard ; seen, " with our eyes "—no mere illusion, but an evident fact that could be "looked upon"; handled—as He said, " handle Me and see ", Luke xxiv. 39 ; John xx. 27. (b) He is personally appropriated by faith. It is not for us to have physical contact with Him now ; but " Blessed are they that have not seen, but yet have believed ", John xx. 29, we may spiritually appropriate Him for ourselves through the medium of the apprehending organ of the spirit—faith, the ear of the soul ; faith, the eye of the soul ; faith, the hand of the soul, that takes Him for our own. So does the " life " come to us through that contact. I Peter ii. 4–5 says, " To whom coming, as unto a living stone . . . ye also, as living stones." Like those electric machines which on your grasping the handles transmit their inherent current into your recipient body. So we have " handled " Him, and we have " life ", and enter the fellowship of those who rejoice in that priceless boon. Look again : this comradeship is also—

A FELLOWSHIP OF LOVE (3)

There is something so joyous about real love ! And we have here a hint of *The Love of Human Fellowship*—" that ye also

may have fellowship with us " (3). Those who, in those
pristine days, had been in physical contact with the Lord had
been drawn together, and bound together, in a bond of mutual
love. Like the spokes of a wheel, being so close to the axle,
they were so near to one another. And now, says the apostle,
not only we who were so close as to touch Him, but " ye also "
may have the joy and strength of this Christian fellowship.
" Blest be the tie that binds our hearts in Christian love."
It was this quality in the relationship between these early
believers that so impressed the onlookers in that rather hard
world, " See how these Christians love one another ! " Oh
that, in place of the bickering and backbiting that occasion-
ally disfigure our Christian behaviour, and stultify our
Christian testimony, the Church at large were to receive, by
the secret given us in Romans v. 5, a new baptism of love, as
in the first days of power. The world would still be impressed
by such a practical evidence of the reality and joy of our
fellowship.

　　Higher, and happier, still is *The Love of Divine Fellowship*—
" and truly our fellowship is with the Father, and with His
Son JESUS CHRIST " (3). How amazing it is that, being what
we are, we receive a welcome into fellowship with Him, being
what He is—the atom consorting with the Almighty ; the
Holy One and the unholy conversing together through the
appointed media of Bible and Prayer. Such godly friendship
has always been open to those who, whatever their circumstances, have been willing to pay the price of utter fidelity
to Him. In a difficult age " Enoch walked with God ",
Genesis v. 22 ; in a degenerate era Noah did the same,
Genesis vi. 9. A like privilege is available to us—on the same
terms !

　　These two fellowships hang together—the one with Him
cementing the other ; the one with them reflecting the other.
A recent correspondent concluded his letter to me, " Yours
because His "—yes, that's right : the inter-dependence of
the dual fellowship. Be it noted that God sets great store by
the fellowship, and warns us against doing any hurt or harm
to it—a Christian, a church-member, failing in love towards
a fellow-believer, acting or speaking in an loving way. That
is a very serious thing, for it is not only the victim that we
hurt, but the Lord Himself, who died for us both. To anyone
who harasses a Christian He would say, " Why persecutest

thou *Me* ? " Acts ix. 4. Note that this blest communion is also—

A FELLOWSHIP OF LIGHT (5-7)

There is something so joyous about clear light !   The verses tell us a part of *The Character of* GOD—who " is light " (5) ; not just " gives "—though He does that, John i. 9—but " is ".   Just as " God is love " (iv. 8, 16), so " God is light " : these qualities are of the very essence of His Being.   Speaking of this passage, Vincent comments that light physically represents glory, intellectually represents truth, and morally represents holiness.   There can be little doubt that, judging from the context, the emphasis here is on the sheer holiness of God.   No careful student of the Bible can fail to observe that there are two facets of the Divine revelation of Himself : (1) the joy of " God is love " ; (2) the Judgment of " God is light ".   These are not contradictory, but complementary, as the late H. S. Guillebaud so clearly brought out in his great little book, *Why the Cross ?* (pp. 60 ff.).   How vividly, and how tragically, the two aspects are brought together in the Saviour's weeping, and warning, over Jerusalem, in Luke xix. 41 ff., and Matthew xxiii. 37-8.   Because He *is* light, " in Him is no darkness at all ".

So it follows that *The Company of* GOD—must be compatible. " Can two walk together except they be agreed ? " asks Amos iii. 3.   Alas, even believers sometimes " *walk in darkness* " (6)—that will not mean that they have forfeited the Life, nor strangled the Love, but that they have beclouded the Light.   They are still in the Family, but they have broken the Fellowship—even as, in a human family, a child's disobedience causes a cloud between him and his father.   How different, how altogether blessed, to " walk . . . in the light of Thy countenance ", Psalm lxxxix. 15 : a sun without cloud or mist.   If we " do not ", it is plain falsehood to claim fellowship.   Ah, but thank God for those who " *walk in the light* " (7)—who live daily in obedience to Him, and rejoice in His way and will.   These know the benediction of the fellowship.   Let it be said that such people have a happy sense of comradeship with other believers—" we have fellowship one with another " ; and also they have a peculiar sensitiveness to sin, and a looking for a continual flow of cleansing—" the blood of JESUS CHRIST, His Son, cleanseth [Gk., goes on cleansing] us from all sin ". Here is a man walking in darkness, because he is blind. In order that he may walk in the light there must first be an initial operation by the ophthalmic surgeon, who will remove the cataract, and then a continual operation of the tear duct, which will keep on cleansing the optic. The first has happened to every believer, when through the glorious saving operation of the Great Surgeon, we can exclaim, in spiritual significance, " One thing I know, that, whereas I was blind, now I see ", John ix. 25. And now, as he walks in the light, that is, walks in obedience, he shall know the continual washing that comes from the precious Blood of CHRIST.

" I am the Light of the world : he that followeth Me shall not walk in darkness but shall have the light of life," says the Master in John viii. 12 ; and, as we have seen, our passage adds, " in Him is no darkness at all " (5). By some law of tenure, it would be possible that, while you possessed an estate, someone else might own a parcel of ground within your demesne, and would have right of way through your part in order to reach his plot, to your discomfort, if he were a disagreeable man. However, the Lord said, " the prince of this world . . . hath nothing in Me ", John xiv. 30 : no darkness at all ! And such is His desire for all His people— " having no part dark ", Luke xi. 36. A dark spot will not only dim the fellowship ; but it may also endanger other lives. In another book I have used a story of W. Y. Fullerton's which I take leave to include here, because it is so germane to what has just been written. It happened in the experience of a lighthouse keeper on the Florida coast. One wild night a pane of glass in his lantern was broken, and not having another to replace it, he substituted for the glass a sheet of tin. That night, they say, a ship was beating up for harbour, and it went ashore with the loss of the ship and of human lives besides. Why ? The light was not extinguished, the light did not burn dim, but there was one part dark ! Is there any such hindrance in us ? Speaking of the darkness of the world around, Philippians ii. 15 says, " Among whom ye shine as lights . . ."—Greek, " luminaries ", lighthouses set for the help of voyagers on the sea of life, warning them of rocks, guiding them to harbour. Well—is there any part dark ? Any bad habit that would led others astray, that would cause shipwreck in another life ?   That would be a grievous blot on the Fellowship.

.   .   .   .   .   .

And now, ere we turn from the passage, let us stay one moment longer on that word " declare ", verse 5—we had it also in verse 3.   It emphasizes the fundamental Christian obligation to tell our discovery to others.   In the world of Medicine, it is part of what is called " The Hippocratic Oath ", which every doctor is supposed to subserve, that he shall, for the benefit of mankind, publish to his brethren any fresh discovery that he may make in the field of medical science. That is one of the differences between the real doctor and the quack—the latter gentleman keeps his discovery to himself, that he may personally batten and fatten upon it.   God grant that we may not be quack Christians, but quick to " declare " what we have found in our fellowship in Him.

> " I hear a clear voice calling, calling
>   Calling out of the night,
> O, you who live in the Light of Life,
>   Bring us the Light !
> We are bound in the chains of darkness,
> Our eyes received no sight,
> O, you who have never been bond or blind,
>   Bring us the Light !
>
> " You cannot—you shall not forget us,
>   Out here in the darkest night,
> We are drowning men, we are dying men,
>   Bring, O, bring us the Light ! "
>   JOHN OXENHAM (*Bees in Amber*.)

It is the Resurrection Commission all over again, as we have it in Matthew xxviii. 6–7—" Come, see . . . go quickly, and tell."

Well, there it is : Life, Love, Light.   What pleasure does such a Fellowship betoken for those who really belong !

II

THE PROBLEM OF THE FELLOWSHIP

I JOHN i. 8–ii. 2

8 If we say that we have no sin, we deceive ourselves, and the truth is not in us.

9 If we confess our sins, he is faithful and just to forgive us *our* sins, and to cleanse us from all unrighteousness.

10 If we say that we have not sinned, we make him a liar, and his word is not in us.

1 My little children, these things write I unto you, that ye sin not. And if any man sin, we have an advocate with the Father, Jesus Christ the righteous ;

2 And he is the propitiation for our sins : and not for ours only, but also for *the sins of* the whole world.

WE saw last time that the threefold mark of the Fellowship, as a body, is that it is a Fellowship of Life, a Fellowship of Love, and a Fellowship of Light. The three notes of the members, as individuals, are Holiness, Happiness, and Helpfulness. We should, if things are right with us, be possessed of those qualities. This section of our Epistle is concerned with the first of them—holiness. The moment we become desirous of this beautiful Christian characteristic, we are made aware of the opposition, we find ourselves sensitive to sin—this it is that is the believer's problem : how to deal with sin.

THE NEED FOR CLEANSING

Yes, Christians ; for it is to such that the Epistle is written —let them learn that, however advanced in holiness they may become, they will never, down here, pass beyond the need for cleansing. Notice here the series of " If's " : each introducing some aspect of the sin problem.

Sin as a Root—" If we say that we have no sin, we deceive ourselves, and the truth is not in us " (8). We are to be careful to distinguish between the root and the fruit—in this verse we are concerned with the former ; and if we were so successful in Christian character and conduct that we had no sinful fruit in our life, we could not truthfully say " we have no sin ", for the root remains, liable to break into fruit at any time. There are those who teach that it is possible to get this ugly root completely extracted—" eradicationists ", they are called. I cannot personally join their company, for I feel that the New Testament is against them, that we Christians have to suffer this evil entail from the Fall, and that the way to deal with the root is not by eradication, but by counteraction. If we think otherwise does not "we deceive ourselves" apply—does this not seem to be the HOLY SPIRIT's teaching, to John here ; and to Paul, in Galatians v. 16–7, " Walk in the SPIRIT, and ye shall not fulfil the lust of the flesh. For the flesh lusteth against the SPIRIT, but (Gk.) the SPIRIT against the flesh. . . ." The flesh, the old sinful nature, the root, always there : the SPIRIT, the counter-acting Divine Agent, for victory.

This evil presence remaining is the reason *why Sin is so Universal.* A jelly-mould gives its pattern to all its children : if you accidently drop something into it, and chip the pattern, all the subsequent jellies will bear the mark of the fall. All those who come from Adam carry the stigma of his Fall. This also explains *why Sin is so Attractive.* There is a some-thing in us that answers to the pull of the temptation without. A magnet will have no effect on a pile of wood-shavings—there is nothing there to respond ; but how different when the approach is to a pile of steel-filings ! There is an element in the steel that finds in the magnet something desirable, and succumbs to its draw. That magnet is like the temptation ; and this root in us finds fascination in it, and yields to its invitation. Here, too, lies the suggestion of *why Sin is so Strong.* This root is like a spy within the castle, in league with the enemy outside, giving increased power to the onslaught, because he knows which doors to leave open. The evil triumvirate of the world, the flesh, and the devil is immensely strengthened by the fact that one of them is hiding within the stronghold itself. In this truth also we have the clue *why Sin is so Usual.* Left to ourselves, we shall always be liable to take the crooked way, and rarely likely to go straight. We are like the " wood " in the game of bowls ; its object will be to lie as close as possible to the little white "jack"—yet, except controlled by the man who knows, it will always go awry. The explanation is, of course, that inside the big wooden ball there is a piece of metal, the "bias", which always gives it a crooked tendency. That wrong bent is overcome by the counteraction of the expert bowler. There it is, then, this problem of indwelling sin (See Romans vii. 20). On the other side we shall lose it ; but while we are this side of glory, we shall always have to reckon with it ; and we shall never be able truthfully to "say that we have no sin" Next, we consider—

Sinfulness as a Character—" our sins, and . . . all unrighteousness " (9). How sadly sinful we are, indeed ! We are not sinners because we sin : we sin because we are sinners in character. A dog is not a dog because it barks : it barks because it's a dog. A tree is not a plum tree because it bears plums : it bears plums because it's a plum tree. Actual sins are the symptoms of the deep-seated malady of a sinful character ; and it is not merely the spots but the disease that the Great Physician would deal with, as we place ourselves in His hands. He will get to the root of the matter : there it is again, the root ! He will remedy matters by implanting Another Root, the SPIRIT, Ephesians v. 9. He will concern Himself not only with sin's characteristics, but with its character.

Is this not the reason why the beginning of the Christian life is so radical in its nature that it has to be described as a New Birth. To become a Christian a man has to be not just a better man, but actually a different man. " Except a man be born again he cannot enter into the kingdom of God ", John iii. 3–5. Suppose a fish wants to become a man— he will not accomplish it by being a better fish : except a fish be born again he cannot enter the Kingdom of man ! " Whosoever shall not receive the Kingdom of God as a little child [that is, by becoming a little child all over again—by being born anew], he shall not enter therein ", Mark x. 15. And as II Corinthians v. 17 has it " If any man be in CHRIST, he is [not a better creature : though he ought also to be that] a new creature "—a " new creation " as the Revised Version puts it. Thus by another, and a new root, it becomes possible to alter the fruit. Now let us look at another aspect of this Sin Problem of ours.

Sinning as a Habit—" If we say that we have not sinned "
(10). Here, says Vincent, is " sin regarded as an act " ; and
that, presumably, not an isolated occasion, but a quite
frequent occurrence. We do, we Christians do, often commit
deeds of ungodliness, and do omit deeds of godliness. Let it
be said specifically that there is no need for this—for, in the
Gospel of full salvation, provision is made for the thwarting
of such unchristian behaviour. Do you think that we all too
often experience failure because we don't expect anything
else ? Did the Master ever deal imperfectly with the physical
ills of men ; and shall it be otherwise when He undertakes the
salvation from spiritual maladies ? Shall not these latter
sufferers also be made " perfectly whole " ? Not " perfect "
yet in the final sense, for the sinful root still remains, but, so
far as present practice is concerned, a complete cure. Such
perfection we may justifiably anticipate—" Be ye therefore
perfect [in your sphere] even as your Father which is in
heaven is perfect [in His sphere] ", Matthew v. 48. Do you
not find this, with the writer, a terribly humbling thought ?
What we should be, and could be, compared with what we
are !

No one, not even the most dastard unbeliever, would dare
to *call* God a liar ; yet some have ventured to " *make* Him a
liar " by professing an immunity from sin which they have
not attained. His word, in Romans iii. 23 for example, says
that " there is no difference, for all have sinned ". A difference
in degree doubtless, but no difference in fact. In a fever ward,
all have the infection but some worse than others. In life, all
have the disease of sin—" there's no difference " as to the
fact ; yet the symptoms, the spots, appear worse in some.
That word of God is in the Scriptures, but " not in us ", if
we deny the truth, and claim to be exempt from the general
accusation.

Sin as a Surprise—is next dealt with. All that the apostle
has been saying is penned in order that his readers may see
the sin problem stated, in our present quotations, and solved,
in our later excerpts—" that ye sin not " (ii. 1). They ought
not, they need not—but what if they do ? " If any man sin "
—there is in that " if " an element of surprise. If he become
guilty of some sin, let it be clearly understood, he is not cast
out of the family, but the fellowship is broken ; just as any
child knows who has been naughty, that the sun goes in

behind a cloud until the sin has been confessed, repented, and forgiven—he has been in the family all the time, but now the fellowship has been restored. "If any man sin"—when the sin comes out, the sun goes in : that's it !

In such an event—we repeat, such a surprising event—let it be remembered that we are not abandoned to our own poor self-efforts at restoration : we have got ourselves into this mess, we must get ourselves out of it. No, no : that would involve us in a helpless, and hopeless, situation. Here is God's way—"we have an Advocate". You are familiar enough with the thought, and, I expect, with the attentions of " your adversary ", I Peter v. 8 ; do we realise sufficiently the boon and blessing of our Advocate—"righteous", in that He Himself has no sin to be dealt with, else He could never have dealt justly and adequately with ours. There He stands in Holy Court, conducting our case before the Righteous Judge, Hebrews ix. 24. We are guilty ; He offers no defence ; but He puts in a plea for mercy, forgiveness and re-instatement —a plea grounded not on my merit (alas, I have none), but on His own : a prevailing propitiation. We shall deal with its nature when we come to study iv. 10. For the moment, we rejoice that it is so gloriously efficacious in settling our case.

What, then, is our wisdom " if any man sin " ? Well, what is our wisdom if we see a lot of water resting upon our knife. Is it not to dry it off at once ? Otherwise, the knife will rust. I recall that, in speaking of ill-gotten gains, James v. 3 says " the rust of them shall be a witness against you." Let us, therefore, as soon as we are conscious of any particular sin, deal with it at once—not waiting even for our evening confession and prayer. Let there be no rust remaining, to blunt the keen edge of our Christian life and testimony. " If any man sin "—surprised into it—seek to get the stain removed without delay. So, from varying aspects, our passage discloses the Need for Cleansing. Think next of—

THE GROUND OF CLEANSING

" The Blood of JESUS CHRIST His son cleanseth us from all Sin " (7). Indeed it is true to say that " the precious Blood of CHRIST ", I Peter i. 19, is the ground, the basis, the foundation of all God's dealings with man, and all God's blessings for man. Nowadays, it is the fashion, in certain circles, to exclude the word from their theological phraseology and hymnody, since they regard it as too crude and too coarse for our modern ears. Yet, even these will not boggle at speaking of the blood of our warriors shed for us on the battlefield. But God didn't hesitate, our Saviour didn't hesitate, Paul didn't hesitate, and now John didn't hesitate—why should you or I hesitate, to speak of it, and that with adoring wonder, with heartfelt gratitude, even with bated breath? Precious is that Blood to God, because it cost Him so much; precious is it to us, because it causes us such blessings. Here, then, is the explanation, and the reason why God is able to grant us the priceless boom of cleansing from sin. Look into the matter more definitely.

" *The Blood of* JESUS CHRIST *His Son* "—so is the cleansing agent described. (*a*) JESUS—the Human name. It is real Blood shed : the Blood of Man for the sin of men. (*b*) CHRIST —the Messianic name. It is the Blood pictured and predicted by that of the GOD-appointed sacrifices of the old Levitical dispensation. In His Blood all those typical sheddings have been fully and finally fulfilled. (*c*) His Son—the Divine description. It is the Blood of Deity, to speak in figure, as we find in Acts xx. 28. No wonder that the shedding is of infinite value ; and no wonder that even the old typical sacrificial blood was held sacred—so that, for instance, when the Israelite houses on Passover night, in Egypt, were blood-sprinkled on the lintel and doorposts, Exodus xii. 7, none was to be on the door-step : it was too holy a thing to be trodden and trampled under foot. That was only the symbol : what shall be said of the reality ? Let us never speak, nor sing, lightly and loosely of the precious Blood—personally, I always write it with a capital " B ".

" *Cleanseth us* "—it may be said that this present tense has a twofold significance. (1) The tense of Competence—the Blood is competent to cleanse, has the property of cleansing. Nothing else can, but this can. You have exactly the same idea in connection with the Old Testament sacrifices. " It is the blood that *maketh* an atonement for the soul ", Leviticus xvii. 11. So it is the Blood that *cleanseth*, that has this property, this efficacy, which belongs to nothing else in all the wide world. Soap and water can clean the outside ; only the Blood can cleanse the heart and conscience within. (2) The tense of Continuance—keeps on cleansing. There is an initial cleansing, when first we " come "; and there is a continual cleansing as often as we come ; and the medium of cleansing is the same, in both cases. I have often heard the illustration as in our first chapter, that it is like the watering of the eye, the flow is always there dealing with the impurities that intrude. Personally, I cannot feel that it is as automatic as that ; but that there must, be, on our part, a continual coming, as often as needs be, in penitence and resolve.

" *From all sin* "—what a sense of completion is conveyed by that word " all ". It is frequently found in the New Testament, and always gives the impression that the matter is complete—there is " all wisdom ", Ephesians i. 8, so that we may always know all we ought to know ; " all joy ", James i. 2, even in the midst of trial and tribulation ; " all patience ", II Corinthians xii. 12, nothing availing to break down our endurance ; " all diligence ", II Peter i. 5, keeping us always busy in the service of GOD, workers and not shirkers ; " all pleasing ", Colossians i. 10, not gratifying self, but Him ; " all might ", Colossians i. 11, so that, whatever our task, our temptation, our testing, we shall have a constant supply of power for continuous victory, which " they which receive . . . shall reign in life ", Romans v. 17. Indeed, what fulness is compressed within the narrow compass of those three (two) little letters—*multum in parvo*. And now we have " all sin ", the HOLY SPIRIT has led John to use the word as comprising all the forms and manifestations of the evil principle. Call sin what you like—evil, corruption, transgression, wickedness, vice, crime, uncleanliness, fall, filth, guilt, bondage, iniquity, stain, wrong, misdemeanour, here are fifteen of its many names and aspects : they are covered by this " all sin ", as a Root, as a Character, as a Habit, as a Surprise. Now consider—

THE RANGE OF CLEANSING

The range is as wide as the need ; and so the whole experience and personality of the believer comes under the blessed process. " Clean every whit " John xiii. 10—is GOD's purpose for His children. A small boy presents himself at the breakfast table—his knees are clean, his hands are clean, his face is clean, even his neck is clean ; but, alas, he is sent upstairs again to complete his ablutions : " You haven't washed behind your ears ! " Our Heavenly Father is not satisfied unless we are clean through and through—and His purpose is always our possibility.

A Cleansed Heart—comes first. " If we confess our sins, He is faithful and just to forgive us our sins, and to cleanse us from all unrighteousness " (9). Take that to pieces. (*a*) " *Confess*—to GOD of course, not to a priest. There may be some occasion when it would be right and salutory for someone weighed down with a sense of sin, under deep conviction, to unburden his soul to some understanding person, with great relief and release ; but for what is known as auricular confession to a priest I can find no warrant in Holy Scripture. Besides the confession to GOD, there must also be, in some instances, confession, and, where practicable, restitution, to the one we have wronged. You will remember how Paul insists on this in the case of the runaway slave and thief, Onesimus, whom he has just led to CHRIST. His master Philemon has, under the then Roman law, absolute power of life or death in such a case—yet Onesimus must take that risk ; he must go back now to Colossæ, and confess his robbery and desertion to the man he has wronged. This is a matter of real importance. It may be that some reader of these lines is failing to know peace in his conscience, and power in his service, simply because, while he has confessed to GOD, he has not put it right (so far as he can) with the one against whom he has sinned. For you, my friend, this may entail a distressing interview, the writing of a difficult letter, but if you would have GOD's best, if you would serve GOD best, it must be done. Are you serious enough, courageous enough, to ask His help and go and do it ? It is this confession to a wronged one that James has in mind when he writes " Confess your faults [note : not your sins] one to another " (v. 16). We are, then, to own up to our sinnership, in general, whether we feel it or not, and to our sins, in particular.

Continue to break up our strategic verse. (*b*) " *Faithful* " —to His promise He will never break His word, concerning anything He has said, and, just now, this thing that He has so lovingly and graciously undertaken to do. " There hath not failed one word of all His good promise ", says I Kings

viii. 56 : no, nor never shall.   I always think that His oft-
repeated promise of His resurrection on the third day was the
strictest test of His fidelity to His word : and I often thrill
at the simple allusion of the angel, " He is risen, as He said ",
Matthew xxviii. 6 : He had said so, and of course He did.
Yes, of course, for He is ever " faithful " to what He has
promised. (c) " *Just* "—to His law. GOD cannot break His
own laws ; and seeing that sin must be righteously dealt
with, and sinners justly punished, Deity, if we may put it so,
had to overcome the problem of how justly to save the sinner.
Everlasing glory be to GOD that His wisdom evolved a plan
wherein His holiness is justified and His love is satisfied—
" CHRIST the power of GOD, and the wisdom of GOD ", I
Corinthians i. 24.   Is His sacrifice in our place a proper
transaction ? Yes, if the Offering is Faultless—as were the
old animals, " without spot or blemish ".   So Pilate says,
" Behold, I bring Him forth to you that you may know that
I find no fault in Him ", John xix. 4 ; Judas confesses, " I
have betrayed the innocent Blood ", Matthew xxvii. 4 ; the
Thief declares, " This Man hath done nothing amiss ", Luke
xxiii. 41 ; the Centurion testifies, " Certainly this was a
righteous Man ", Luke xxiii. 47.   If He had had sin of His
own, He could not righteously be accepted for ours ; but GOD
" hath made Him who knew no sin to be sin for us ", II
Corinthians v. 21.   Just ? Yes, if the Sacrifice is Voluntary—
" I lay down My life . . . no man taketh it from Me, but I
lay it down of Myself ", John x. 17–8.   A willing Victim was
He.   Just ? Yes, if the Substitution is Adequate—a Man in
place of another man, even in place of all other men : is that
right and fair ?   No, but you see although He was really
man, He was not merely man.   Deity was conjoined with
Humanity, and that gives peculiar significance, and adequate
sufficiency, to His acting as Substitute for all.   " If Thou be
the Son of GOD "—said His enemies, at Golgotha, Matthew
xxvii. 40.   " Truly this *was* the Son of GOD "—said the
soldiers, verse 54.   Thus was His atoning death for us a just
proceeding : so much so that it would be thoroughly unjust
if GOD did not pardon a penitent sinner.

   And now, further (d) " *To forgive . . . and to cleanse* "—
these verbs are, in the Greek, in the aorist tense, which
indicates that they are implemented definitely and decisively
in a specific moment of time.   The necessity for any subsequent

cleansing will emerge in our next paragraph ; but this original and eternal benefit becomes ours the moment we believe. So, by the infinite mercy and grace of GOD, we receive a cleansed heart—

> " Oh, for a heart to praise my God,
>   A heart from sin set free ;
>   A heart that's sprinkled with the Blood
>   So freely shed for me."

But that does not exhaust the range of this beneficent operation.

A Cleansed Walk—" These things write I unto you, that ye sin not " (ii. 1).   Here we are to grasp the difference between Bathing and Rinsing which our Lord taught His disciples by that striking parable in action, in the Upper Room—" He that is washed needeth not save to wash his feet ", John xiii. 10. The two words here rendered " wash " are different words in the original, and would be more exactly translated " bathing " and " rinsing " respectively, as above.   The bathing represents that original whole cleansing which we received when first we trusted CHRIST, without which " thou hast no part with " Him (8).   At which the impulsive disciple exclaims, " Not my feet only, but also my hands and my head " (9).   No, no, Peter—that over-all bath needs no repeating : the first and fundamental cleansing suffices for all eternity ; but there *is* necessity for day-to-day purifying from the dust, and dirt, and defilement of the way.   Peter, reader, not your whole being again—but " your feet ", your walk ; and by the same blessed agency of " the Blood ".   Seek this blest rinsing at the close of each day, if you have not found need for it even before.   So the range of cleansing widens.

A Cleansed Account—" we have an Advocate with the Father, JESUS CHRIST, the righteous " (ii. 1).   GOD has, in His mysterious providence, allowed " the accuser of our brethren ", Revelation xii. 10, to enter the Court of Heaven against us, as in the case of Job, i. 6, and Joshua, the High Priest, Zechariah iii. 1 ; but " we have an Advocate ", as we considered earlier in this present Study.   Have you come across that beautiful bit of type-history in Nehemiah xi. 24, " Pethahiah was at the king's hand in all matters concerning the people " ?   Artaxerxes, following upon the policy of Darius, had allowed a number of the captive Jews to return to their own land, specially to build up the broken-down walls of their beloved Jerusalem. He was always interested in them, and concerned for their welfare ; and he arranged for Pethahiah, one of themselves, to remain at Court, to be always available for Jewish matters. If His Majesty wanted information relating to the life and circumstances of the people, he could always obtain it first-hand from their representative. On the other hand, if they had some request, some need, they could always approach the king through their advocate " in all matters ". What a beautiful picture of our Advocate, one of ourselves, made like unto His brethren, "now to appear in the presence of GOD for us ", Hebrews ix. 24. We have a Heavenly Pethahiah ; and we can make our supplications, and obtain our supplies thus " through JESUS CHRIST our Lord ". He represents us there, and presents our petition—be it for Power, for Purity, for Pleasure, for Plenty, or, as in the instance of our particular passage, for Pardon. So we may rejoice in a Cleansed Account, through the mediacy and advocacy of Him Who shed His Blood not only to Make but also to Keep us clean. If we may vary the metaphor, in contrast to our financial position at the bank, it is good, in this spiritual record, always to have our account " in the red "—under the Blood. And now it is full time to close up this present Study with a final brief word about—

THE MESSAGE OF CLEANSING

" He is the propitiation for our sins ; and not for ours only but also for the sins of the whole world " (ii. 2). The Bible never allows us to forget others. We who know the Joyful News are under strict obligation to pass it on to other needy souls. " Let the redeemed of the LORD say so ", Psalm cvii. 2, still is in force. Would that we were all like Naaman's little maid, who knew where her leprous master could find cleansing, and who did not—from innate shyness, nor for fear of being ridiculed, nor in sheer indifference—refrain from telling what she knew. " Would GOD my lord were with the prophet that is in Samaria, for he would recover him of his leprosy ", II Kings v. 3. Be ours, then, the happy privilege of telling those stricken with the dread leprosy of sin of the " fountain opened . . . for sin and for uncleanness ", Zechariah xiii. 1, even from " these wounds in Thine hands " (verse 6).

> " E'er since by faith I saw the stream
> Thy flowing wounds supply,
> Redeeming love has been my theme,
> And shall be till I die."

III

THE PASSION OF THE FELLOWSHIP

I JOHN ii. 3-11

3 And hereby we do know that we know him, if we keep his commandments.

4 He that saith, I know him, and keepeth not his commandments, is a liar, and the truth is not in him.

5 But whoso keepeth his word, in him verily is the love of God perfected : hereby know we that we are in him.

6 He that saith he abideth in him ought himself also so to walk, even as he walked.

7 Brethren, I write no new commandment unto you, but an old commandment which ye had from the beginning. The old commandment is the word which ye have heard from the beginning

8 Again, a new commandment I write unto you, which thing is true in him, and in you : because the darkness is past, and the true light now shineth.

9 He that saith he is in the light, and hateth his brother, is in darkness even until now.

10 He that loveth his brother abideth in the light, and there is none occasion of stumbling in him.

11 But he that hateth his brother is in darkness, and walketh in darkness, and knoweth not whither he goeth, because that darkness hath blinded his eyes.

THAT passion can be put into one word : Loyalty. Our very membership commits us to certain loyalties. When you come to think about it, belonging to any organisation involves standing by its regulations and constitution ; and that is no less the case when we come to belong to the Christian fellowship. And when anyone is a really keen member, his loyalties begin to be something of a passion with him. We had better note, in starting, that phrase, " He that saith ", which comes three times over in this section—verses 4, 6, and 9 ; for it is around that phrase that the loyalties are discussed. It is our duty to say ; but it is not enough to say. Well now, let us consider, first, our pre-eminent obligation—

LOYALTY TO THE HEAD OF THE FELLOWSHIP

What is it that is here said ?—" I know Him " (4). It is the fact that in our relationship with Him, as that between

ourselves and others, there are degrees of acquaintance.
(a) *Introduction*—when we are first brought into touch with
Him, as our Saviour and Lord : as was Peter when Andrew
introduced them, John i. 42. Do you, my reader, know Him
thus far ? No question in life, on earth, could be of greater
moment for an unconverted sinner. What, then, say you ?
(b) *Increase*—when, day by day, we are brought into closer
touch with Him, as our Master and Teacher : as was Peter
when, as one of the Twelve, JESUS " ordained twelve, that
they should be with Him, and that He might send them
forth. . . ." Mark iii. 14. For us, that growing acquaintance
is acquired by the daily listening to His voice in His Word,
by the habitual speaking to Him in prayer at His footstool,
by the regular frequenting with Him at His table, by the
consistent walking with Him in a life of plain, simple obedience. (c) *Intimacy*—we are immensely privileged to live in
closest fellowship with Him, as our greatest Friend : as was
Peter, when, with other two, he was graciously allowed to
accompany his LORD to the heights of revelation, in the
Transfiguration, Mark ix. 2, to the heights of wonder, in the
Raising to New Life, Mark v. 37, to the heights of privilege,
in the Garden, Mark xiv. 33. Let it be said that JESUS has
no favourites, but He has intimates—and you, or I, can be
one of them, if we are willing to pay the cost, the full implications of John xv. 14's " whatsoever ". Well then, do you
say, " I know Him " ; and to what degree do you know Him ?
Wherein, further, shall be found the token of your true
loyalty to Him ?

Obedience is the Test—" He that saith, I know Him, and
keepeth not His commandments, is a liar, and the truth is
not in him " (4). How scathing John can be—this apostle
of love ! Just like his Master—Whose gentle lips gave
forth those scarifying utterances of Matthew xxiii, the Wrath
of the Lamb ; yet Who closed that terrible chapter with the
poignantly pathetic words of the verse 37, " O Jerusalem,
Jerusalem, how often would I have gathered thy children
together, even as a hen gathereth her chickens under her
wings, and ye would not ". Conversely, as another indication
of the two aspects of the Master's nature, you have the strange
contrast, " Behold, the Lion . . . and I beheld, and lo . . .
a Lamb ", Revelation v. 5–6. John, too, could shew that
sterner side, when " the truth " required it. Indeed, it was

that harder side that had previously predominated, as you can see by the nickname that our Lord gave him and his brother James, " Boanerges, sons of thunder ", Mark iii. 17. But long since all that has changed, the HOLY SPIRIT, of Whom He spoke so much in chapters xiv and xvi of his Gospel, had done the transforming work in his own heart. He who once proposed to call down fire from heaven, Luke ix. 54, was now concerned for the fire of the HOLY GHOST—to burn out the dross of sin, and to burn in the pattern of love. It is not for nothing that Isaiah iv. 4 describes Him as " a Spirit of burning ". Day by Day obedience, then, is the Test of our real, sincere knowledge of Him.

Obedience is a Measure—" whoso keepeth His word, in him verily is the love of GOD perfected " (5). If doing what He says is a test of whether we truly know Him, the same token is also a measure of how much we love Him. It is no use a little child saying that she loves mother very much if she doesn't do what mother tells her. A like attitude shall determine what degree of love we really have for our Heavenly Father—whether merely incipient ; or whether expanding ; or whether fulll-grown, or " perfect ", as it is called here. Fine-grade obedience, full-grown love : the two go together, hand and glove. We sometimes think of our LORD'S words in John xiv. 15, " If ye love Me, keep My commandments ", as a command, and we are so justified with the Authorised Version before us ; but it is more correctly given in the Revised Version as a plain, simple statement of the bare truth—" If ye love Me, ye *will* keep My commandments ". Of course you will ! In the passage that we are studying, the word " keepeth " is a present tense, whose implication is, not just a single, big act of obedience, but a continuous activity of plain every-day obedience—in little things as well as in big things ; in material things as well as in spiritual things ; in secret things as in open things. " Whatsoever He saith unto you, do it ", John ii. 5—even though it be such a little insignificant thing as filling a jar with water—and His blessing shall be upon the obedience.

We Evangelicals have placed such emphasis upon the duty and efficacy of Trust—and we cannot stress this too much—that we have sometimes appeared to underline too little the paramount importance of Obedience. Yet, James, and Paul, and John, and even the Master Himself, all, in various ways, combine to teach us that the two go together—the two legs on which we progress heavenwards, the two hands in which we receive Divine blessing, the two knees on which we practice effectual prayer, the two eyes with which we discern the unclouded vision of spiritual truth, the two ears which enable us clearly to hear the voice of GOD in His word, the two lips with which we may the more effectively declare the gospel of His grace. Think those similes out, and see how truly they do indicate the dual office performed for us by Trust and Obedience in all spiritual experience and advance. The old chorus was exactly right which said, " Trust and obey, for there's no other way, To be happy in JESUS (to be anything in JESUS), but to trust and obey ". All which we have appended to our consideration of the portion of Scripture now in our minds in order to sharpen in our spiritual perspective the essential quality of Obedience—the Test of our Know-. ledge, the measure of our Love, the token of our Loyalty to the Divine Head of our Fellowship. Next comes—

LOYALTY TO THE RULE OF THE FELLOWSHIP

What is it that is here said ?—" He abideth in Him " (6). As John records in chapter xv. of his Gospel, our LORD chose a very familiar process of nature in order to press home the fundamental necessity for a believer to " abide " in Him. So close is the relationship that He likens Himself to the Vine, and us to the Branches. Our sharing of the Sap of the HOLY SPIRIT, and our consequent bearing of the Fruit of the SPIRIT, Galatians v. 22-3, depend upon our abiding in the Vine—as He explained in verse 5, " without Me [that is, apart from Me] ye can do nothing " : nothing in the way of fruit, nor in the way of any Christian excellence.

As the token of our first loyalty was the law of obedience, so the mark here is the law of imitation—" He that saith he abideth in Him ought himself also so to walk, even as He walked ". That is the rule, almost the slogan, of the Fellow-ship—" walk as He walked ". That is the outward sign that we are abiding in CHRIST.

The Imitation must be kept in the right Order. It is quite useless to tell anyone who is not a Christian to imitate CHRIST. Even if he could, it would not make him a Christian, any more than an ape aping a man, however cleverly, makes the monkey a man. But, in any case, the non-Christian cannot imitate Him. He must take Him first as his Saviour before he can make Him his Exemplar—otherwise you might as well tell a chair to " walk ", as tell a man still " dead in trespasses and sins ", Ephesians ii. 1, " to walk, even as He walked ". True, I Peter ii. 21 tells us of the Master leaving us an example, " that ye should follow His steps ", but we recall that Peter's Epistles, like all the New Testament Letters, were addressed to Christians—first Christian, then Christ-like : that is the right order.

The Imitation must be regulated in the right Manner. Says old Martin Luther, " It is not CHRIST walking on the sea, but His ordinary walk, that we are called on here to imitate "— yes, in the common ways of life. The little steps of Childhood as He went holding His Mother's hand ; the bigger steps of Boyhood, as " He went down with them to Nazareth, and was subject unto them ", Luke ii. 51 ; the longer strides of Manhood, as He " went about doing good ", Acts x. 38 ; the purposeful tread of Saviourhood, as He " steadfastly set His face to go to Jerusalem ", Luke ix. 51, as we go through the sacred story, we find His example set before us on every page, in every age, at every stage. And the rule is—as He, so we ! It is the safe rule in life—not to follow other people's example : they may, though inadvertently, let you down, and lead you astray. It is like regulating your watch by another man's, when all the while his may be fast or slow. Better is it to go by Greenwich Mean Time. So, not what would others think, say, do ; but what would JESUS do ? There are, of course, circumstances of our modern life that did not fall within His human experience ; but, even so, the way He acted then, the spirit He shewed, will pretty well indicate how He would be likely to meet the conditions of our day. So we may very happily finish this paragraph with the twofold prayer of a very practical poet of long ago, " Teach me the way . . . make me to go ", Psalm cxix. 33–5, which will lead us straight into our next thought : How are we to go His way, to do His will ?

The Imitation can be achieved in the right Strength. That word " ought " is often a great comfort to me—because " o–u–g–h–t " spells " Can " ! My scriptural warrant for that is in Exodus xviii. 23, " If . . . GOD command thee so . . . thou shalt be able to ". No one will deny that we *ought* to do His will : in that case, let no one doubt that we *can*. And now He says to us through Paul, " Be ye therefore imitators of GOD as dear children ", Ephesians v. 1, R.V. The Greek word for " followers ", " imitators ", is that from which our English word " mimics " is derived—what mimics the " dear children " are ! As children, then, of the Heavenly Father, let this loyalty to the Rule of our Fellowship, to be increasingly like Him, be an integral part of the Passion of our lives. And now, a third area of the passion must occupy our serious attention—

LOYALTY TO THE MEMBERS OF THE FELLOWSHIP

What is it that is here said ?—" He is in the light " (9). Well, we shall not just take his word for it ; we shall soon find out if it is really true. The law of love will test the matter. The apostle maintains this figure of light and darkness as representing love and hate.

Hatred is of the very kingdom of Darkness. What a terrible picture is given us of the man who hates another. (*a*) *He lives in the dark*—" is in darkness even until now " (9). You know what would happen to a flower if it were kept in the dark. Oh yes, it would grow ; but it would lose all its beautiful colour, and would come forth a dull, drab thing. Few things make a soul so ugly as a spirit of hatred, an unforgiving, unloving attitude towards another. Dark : what a place to live in ! (*b*) *He walks in the dark*—" walketh in darkness, and knoweth not whither he goeth " (11). That is, doesn't know where it will lead him—his vicious thoughts may lead to violent deeds. John will say presently, iii. 15, " whosoever hateth his brother is a murderer ". You never can tell. These vengeful feelings lay seeds that may grow to odious fruitage. (*c*) *He gropes in the dark*—" darkness hath blinded his eyes " (11). Such is the inevitable result of perpetually living and walking in the dark—as may be seen in the case of the poor little pit ponies that were used (now largely displaced by machinery) in the coal-mines ; there are blind fish swimming about in the darkness of certain subterranean waters. So is this deluded man blind—he can't see reason ; he can't recognise truth ; he can't find any safety : except in the sincere utterance of a prayer that was blessedly honoured long, long ago, " Lord, that I may receive my sight ", Luke xviii. 41.

Love is of the very Kingdom of Light. How gladsome to turn from the dreariness of the preceding paragraph. All now is completely different. " The true light now shineth " (8)— because you let into your heart and life Him Who said, " *I am* the Light of the world ", John viii. 12 ; and now, reflecting Him to others, you have been fulfilling His purpose for your life, " *Ye are* the light of the world ", Matthew v. 14. If that is really so, there is one thing, anyhow, that I know about you—you live in a spirit of love and loyalty to all the members of the Fellowship. This law of love is " an old commandment " (7), not simply new—it was inculcated " from the beginning ", that is, of the Gospel. It was an elementary, primary Lesson in the School of CHRIST. It was so obviously and regularly practiced that, as we quoted earlier, even the surrounding pagans had to say, " See how these Christians love one another ". But this law is also " a new commandment " (8), not only old—since it is freshly enunciated, from age to age, and even from day to day : the light of each new morning brings happy reminder of the love that is to characterise the succeeding hours. So the passage has much to tell us about this joyous man. (*a*) *He lives in the light*—" abideth in the light " (10). Just as he who dwells in sunny climes, or even spends a summer fortnight by the shining sea, bears the imprint of his dwelling upon his very countenance, so he who abides in Eternal Light cannot but wear the impress upon his whole behaviour and demeanour. Do you know that American Revised Version of Psalm xxxiv. 5, " They looked unto Him, and were radiant " ? That's it : the radiance of love. (*b*) *He walks in the light*—" there is none occasion of stumbling in him " (10). This man, unlike his unfortunate counterpart, is able to see the pitfalls in his path, and may thus, if he so wills, avoid them. Moreover, he is in a position to refrain from leaving stumbling-blocks for others. I remember the late beloved Bishop Taylor Smith telling us of an occasion when he was walking up and down a railway station platform, waiting for a train. Thinking of some matter, he carelessly trod on a piece of orange peel, and almost fell : not looking, not, as it were, walking in the light, he met with an occasion of stumbling. Walking on, the Bishop had a sudden, happy inspiration : he went back, and kicked the peel off on to the track, thus ensuring that he should not leave behind him a stumbling-block for others !

"Which thing "—this law of love—" is true in Him, and in you " (8). *In Him*—how gloriously conspicuous it was, as He trod the ways of men, and still is, as He intercedes for us above. Do you know that vivid poem of Charles Wesley's, on " Wrestling Jacob ", with its concluding stanzas—

> " Contented now upon my thigh
>   I halt, till life's short journey end ;
> All helplessness, all weakness I,
>   On Thee alone for strength depend,
> Nor have I power, from Thee, to move ·
>   Thy nature, and Thy name is Love.

> " Lame as I am, I take the prey,
>   Hell, earth, and sin with ease o'ercome ;
> I leap for joy, pursue my way,
>   And as a bounding hart fly home,
> Thro' all eternity to prove
>   Thy nature, and Thy name is Love."

In you—how daily evident it should also be, because He " hath called you out of darkness into His marvellous light ", I Peter ii. 9.

Here, then, we close this Meditation on the believers' threefold passion : Loyalty to the Head—in the law of Obedience ; Loyalty to the Rule—in the law of Imitation ; Loyalty to the Members—in the law of Love. May we all be thus utterly loyal members of this Divine Fellowship.

IV

THE PROGRESS OF THE FELLOWSHIP

<u>I JOHN ii. 12–14</u>

12 I write unto you, little children, because your sins are forgiven you for his name's sake.

13 I write unto you, fathers, because ye have known him *that is* from the beginning. I write unto you, young men, because ye have overcome the wicked one. I write unto you, little children, because ye have known the Father.

14 I have written unto you, fathers, because ye have known him *that is* from the beginning. I have written unto you, young men, because ye are strong, and the word of God abideth in you, and ye have overcome the wicked one.

THE entrance to the Fellowship is not a stopping place, but a starting place—as in all life, there is to be growth, progress. Some people miss so much for lack of this onward spirit. Like the poor woman who, trudging wearily through the driving rain and icy wind, came at last to the big house for which she was bound. When the door was opened to her she found a great blazing fire in the grate. On the door re-closing she sank down on the mat inside, utterly worn out, and wet through. Get up, they said, and come to the fire and get dry and warm. No, she answered, don't disturb me, I'm quite content to remain here. Now that you are in the Fellowship, are you content to stay on the mat ? Psalm lxxxiv. 10 says, " I had rather be a door-keeper in the house of my GOD than to dwell in the tents of wickedness ", where the rendering of the opening phrase would legitimately be, " I would rather be just inside the door. . . ." Yes, of course, better be only just inside than be left outside ; but why stick there and miss all the blessings open to those who venture farther and farther on in the Christian life. I sometimes recall the old refrain

> " More and more, more and more,
> Still there's more to follow.
> Have you on the Lord believed.
> Still there's more to follow."

The poetry is negligible ; the fact is immeasurable. There is even danger, as well as loss, in failing to get on. A little fellow had been tucked in to bed, but, after a bit, had fallen out. When mother came running upstairs to see what had happened, and asked however he had fallen out, the child said, " I don't know, mummie, unless it was I went to sleep too near where I got in." Ah, how many Christians have done that. It's asking for a fall !

The New Testament is full of this idea of progress. Look at Hebrews vi. 1, "Leaving the principles . . . let us go on unto perfection ; not laying again the foundation. . . ." That doesn't mean throwing the first things overboard but leaving them there as you do the foundations when you are building a house : you don't need to lay the foundation again, it's there—now " let us go on ", till we reach the completed edifice. Look at Colossians ii. 6-7, " As ye have received CHRIST JESUS the LORD, so walk ye in Him, rooted, and built up in Him ". There, by the threefold variation of his metaphor, the apostle impresses upon his Christian readers the importance of their spiritual growth : the progress of a walk, the progress of a tree, the progress of a house. And now we have John, by the means of yet another illustration, pointing the same salutory lesson—some have grown in spiritual stature to be as " Fathers " ; some are spiritually vigorous " Young Men " ; some, for all their physical age, are yet " Little children " in grace.

He begins with a general and inclusive remark, embracing all believers, and calling them all " little children "—a different word in the Greek from that used in verse 13. The reason here seems to lie between one or other of two explanations. (a) He is by now an old man, and is in the habit of addressing younger people by this title, as ancients often do. (b) He is writing particularly for those who, as a matter of fact, are his children in the faith—so he uses this affectionate, fatherly, family name. Note how he adds " your sins are forgiven you for His Name's sake " (12). That is true of every real believer, of whatever age, the oldest, or the youngest, in GOD's family. We are, indeed, never in the Family unless, or until, that has happened. Oh, the bliss of it, that what we have done as sinners, is forgiven for the sake of what He has done, as Saviour. We repeat, this is true of all Christians, however long or short a time we have been such.

" You Fathers "

You notice that, led as he is by the HOLY SPIRIT, John begins at the top. Is there, I wonder, anything deliberate about that ? Is it that GOD is concerned to place the highest, the greatest, before us at the start before He contemplates for us anything less than the best ? Would He have us fix our eyes on the peak of spiritual attainment that we may the more readily overcome the obstacles on the way thitherward ; would He have our minds filled at the outset with a Divine discontent with anything lower than His highest ? Aspire, then, to be " fathers ", with as rapid progress as may be.

" *Ye have known Him that is from the beginning* " (13-4). Twice the description is given. It refers, I think, to the knowledge of CHRIST, as in the opening of his Gospel (i. 1), and as in the opening of this Epistle (i. 1). " Known " is an elastic word, meaning much or little according to the context. In our last Study we spoke of the growth in that knowledge— these " fathers " are to be presumed to know much, and to know intimately. They will thus have become aware of (*a*) *His Mind*—what He thinks about things ; what He purposes about things. They will be conscious of (*b*) *His Heart*—so filled with love for sinful men, Romans v. 8, even while hating their sin. They will possess an instinct for (*c*) *His Best* —in what His children may have, and be, and do.

How immensely fruitful is such knowledge of Him. Paul places it in the very forefront of his deep desire for spiritual understanding. " That I may know . . . the power of His ' resurrection ' ", the life of the Risen One activating in him. Yes, wonderful ! " That I may know . . . the fellowship of His suffering, being made conformable unto His death ", his self crucified with CHRIST. Yes, wonderful ! But, firstly, and chiefly, " that I may know *Him* ", Philippians iii. 10. Paul longs increasingly (do we ?), not merely for knowledge of deeper blessing, richer experience—though he will not undervalue these — but for ever deepening, ever closer, acquaintance with his Divine Saviour, Master, Friend. What constraining impetus lies there. See it, for instance, in Daniel xi. 32, " The people that do know their GOD shall be strong, and do exploits "—such knowledge moves the heart, steels the will, nerves the arm, to adventure for GOD. Ned

Weeks, a man uneducated and ungifted, but with a heart aflame with love for GOD and for men, did such a remarkable work in the town of Northampton that they gave him a public funeral, when crowds lined the streets with every evidence of real sorrow as the cortege passed. A stranger standing by, on asking who this was, and why all this demonstration, was given, in the rough vernacular, the explanation, " You see, he was wonderful thick wiv' the Almighty." Ah yes, he knew Him. To be educated—grand ; to be gifted—grand ; to be enthusiastic—grand ; but grandest of all is to " know Him ", for this will over-rule any disability, caused through no fault of our own, and enable us to dare and do for Him.

This, then, is the supreme mark of " the fathers ", the essential qualification for spiritual parenthood. What a joy it is to have spiritual children, those whom we have been enabled to lead to CHRIST. How Paul rejoiced in being able to speak of Timothy as " my own son in the faith ", and as " my dearly beloved son " (I. i. 2 ; II. i. 2), and of " my son Onesimus " (Philemon 10). And with what fatherly delight John writes " I have no greater joy than to hear my children walk in truth " (III. 4). Covet to be thus a " father ", or mother, of many—so to know GOD that you may be able to lead others to know Him.

" YOU YOUNG MEN "

These Christians are not yet at the top ; but they are climbing steadily, and by the look of it they are not so very far off. John has more to say—and very delightful things, too —about this stage of spiritual attainment than the other two. Perhaps these latter are more simply conceived—the beginning of the life, the closing of the life ; while those in the middle reaches are more beset with problems. What a famous Scottish preacher, the late Dr. G. H. Morrison, called " The Perils of Middle Age ", when preaching on Psalm xci. 6, " The destruction that wasteth at noonday ". Certainly our young men and women of to-day have more difficulties and dangers to face in these times than were ever our lot yesterday. The whole atmosphere of life is different. Yet, having said that, one reflects upon what was the atmosphere of the world in which these early Christian " young men " were called to

live their life and give their testimony. They did it by the
same secret as Christian young men can do it still—"not I,
but CHRIST liveth in me", Galatians ii. 20. But, in returning
to our passage, we recall to mind that the people to whom
John writes are, one imagines, not literal young men, but
believers of any age who are young in the faith, who have
all the vitality, exuberance, and adventurousness of youth
exhibited in their Christian living. Older or not in years,
they have a freshness and virility and enthusiasm that
proclaims them as the young men and women of the Kingdom.
Mark some of their outstanding qualifications.

" *Ye have overcome the wicked one* " (13)—they have under-
gone many temptations, but overcome them; indeed,
recognising that behind every inducement to sin there lies
lurking the sinister personality of "the wicked one", with
all the hosts of evil spirits at his beck and call, Ephesians vi.
12, they combat not merely it, but him. There are those who
deny the personality of the devil; but not so did the Master,
the account of Whose wilderness conflict opens with the
words, "when the tempter [not just the temptation] came to
Him . . ." Matthew iv. 3. Many a contest with the Satanic
myrmidons had these "young men" waged, and many a
victory they had gained. You see, there is a secret of victory
which these had learned—and we shall learn it in a later
Study of this very Epistle. It is, alas, sadly true that many
third-rate, poor-grade, Christians are living defeated lives:
such an unsatisfactory thing for themselves, such a bad
example to others, such a poor advertisement for the faith.
How different are those spoken of by Paul, in Romans v. 17,
that "they which receive abundance of grace . . . shall
reign in life". Reign, not over people nor kingdoms, but
over feelings, and fears, and circumstances, and habits, and
sins. You see, these "young men" are triumphant over-
comers, because—

" *Ye are strong* " (14)—a weak Christian is a contradiction
in terms, for the purposes of GOD never contemplate such a
thing. Unfortunately, there are not a few delicate, invalid
Christians; and all such should attend at once the Great
Physician's clinic, to discover what is wrong, and to get
things put right. Among the common symptoms of this
spiritual debility are (*a*) A lack of good food—seen in the
fact of no appetite for the Word; (*b*) A lack of good, fresh

air—the mountain breezes that blow about the footstool of prayer ; (c) A lack of good exercise—in the service of GOD. Nowhere is it more certain that idleness is the precursor of illness. How frequently, in both Testaments, do the Scriptures exhort us to " Be strong "—whether in Joshua i. 9, 18, Haggai ii. 4 ; or in Ephesians vi. 10. Wherefore, let us heed the injunction, not only for our sake, but for others, since " we that are strong ought to bear the infirmities of the weak ", Romans xv. 1. The description proceeds—

" *The Word of God abideth in you* " (14)—here is one of the big secrets for the development of moral muscle and spiritual sinew. All big Christians have been Bible Christians ; all who have been greatly blessed to others have been themselves steeped in it. I read in Acts xviii. 24 of Apollos, that he was " mighty in the Scriptures "—that was, of course, only the Old Testament, and he had much to learn of New Testament truth ; but what he possessed possessed him, so that, out of his knowledge of the Sacred Writing, he was able, with eloquence, and with fervent enthusiasm, to teach and help many. Such a grasp of the Bible is not to be acquired easily, or quickly ; to begin the day with the, sometimes hurried, reading of the day's portion is not enough—it is good so far as it goes, but it doesn't go far enough. Time must be found, and stuck to, for a regular weekly period of real study in some selected Book or Subject—so that gradually we begin to grasp the Bible, and the Bible begins to grip us. I note again that " the Word . . . abideth " in these virile Christians—it lives there ! With some it pays but a brief fleeting visit — that five or ten minutes in the morning, and then off again till next day ; but with these it has come to take up its residence in them. They have given it such a welcome that it has come to stay. It has become part of themselves. It is always there to consult, to advise, to cheer. Something of this sense lies behind Paul's exhortation in Colossians iii. 16, " Let the word of CHRIST dwell in you richly in all wisdom, teaching and admonishing . . . with grace in your hearts. . . ." How that verse reminds me of the late Mr. George Goodman—of ever blessed memory. Often have I heard him at a Question Hour ; and always he would begin his answer with a Scripture quotation—the Word dwelling in him richly. And what grace was in his heart ! And now—

"You Little Children"

Here is the different word from that used in verse 12—that being the generic title used by John for all the children of GOD, this the specific name given by him to all who have only just been "born again", or who have not grown in grace since that day. This particular word is used only on one other occasion, in verse 20, one of whose striking implications we shall note presently.

"*Ye have known the Father*"—does it appear strange that the same characteristic is singled out for these as is predicated of the "fathers" (13)—that of knowledge? I think not, when you recollect that this quality is, as we have seen, of an ever-growing nature. It is noteworthy that whereas the "fathers" are said to know CHRIST, as we so interpret it, the "little children" are stated to love the Father. But, after all, the statement is close to child psychology, for the little thing, while scarcely aware of other people, has at a very early age a knowledge of Daddy and Mummy. That is a very lovely thing that Paul has in Galatians iv. 6, "Because ye are sons, GOD hath sent forth the SPIRIT of His Son into your hearts, crying Abba, Father"—the HOLY SPIRIT teaching the babe in CHRIST to lisp his first word: the Aramaic word "Abba" does not need teeth to pronounce it! The child in faith does begin to know his Heavenly Father—not as his senior knows Him, but he does know Him in his measure. He knows Him as the One to Whom he must look for all supplies, and all sufficiencies.

I draw your attention to a remarkable statement lower down in this chapter, verse 20, "Ye have an unction from the Holy One, and ye know all things". That will presumably be said concerning the "fathers"?—No, although it would be true of them. Concerning the "young man", then—No, although it would be true of them also. It is actually used of the "little children" in the faith. To paraphrase the version, without violating the truth: You, even you Christian children, have the HOLY SPIRIT within you, and you are thus in a position to get to know all things that it is necessary to know for your spiritual well-being and well-doing. Yes, even the little children in grace—for the word here is the one used elsewhere only in verse 13. The fact is that every believer, whatever be his grade of spiritual growth, has open to him this inexhaustible source of information and inspiration to fit the demands of his conditions and circumstances. Even the youngest, in knowing the Father, may know all that is needful.

Oh, then, to be continually growing in the uninterrupted progress of the Fellowship. To the just converted He says, " As new-born babes, desire the sincere [unadulterated] milk of the Word, that ye may grow thereby ", I Peter ii. 2. To the unsatisfactory Christians, who are making no progress, He says, " I have fed you with milk [still], and not with meat : for hitherto ye were not able to bear it, neither yet now are ye able ", I Corinthians iii. 2. To those who are happily going on with GOD He says, " From a child thou hast known the Holy Scriptures, which are able to make thee wise unto salvation through faith which is in CHRIST JESUS . . . and [are] profitable for doctrine, for reproof, for correction, for instruction in righteousness, that the man of GOD may be perfect [full-grown], throughly furnished unto all good works ", II Timothy iii. 15–7. How dependent we all are upon the Word of GOD, the importance of whose study we stressed on an earlier page.

We cannot close this Meditation without referring to the all-round progress of our LORD in His earthly life. " And JESUS increased in wisdom and stature, and in favour with GOD and man ", Luke ii. 52. That is, He grew [as Man] mentally, and physically, and spiritually, and socially.

V

THE PERILS OF THE FELLOWSHIP

15 Love not the world, neither the things *that are* in the world. If any man love the world, the love of the Father is not in him.

16 For all that *is* in the world, the lust of the flesh, and the lust of the eyes, and the pride of life, is not of the Father, but is of the world.

17 And the world passeth away, and the lust thereof : but he that doeth the will of God abideth for ever.

18 Little children, it is the last time : and as ye have heard that antichrist shall come, even now are there many antichrists ; whereby we know that it is the last time.

19 They went out from us, but they were not of us : for if they had been of us, they would *no doubt* have continued with us : but *they went out*, that they might be made manifest that they were not all of us.

20 But ye have an unction from the Holy One, and ye know all things.

21 I have not written unto you because ye know not the truth, but because ye know it, and that no lie is of the truth.

22 Who is a liar but he that denieth that Jesus is the Christ ? He is antichrist, that denieth the Father and the Son

23 Whosoever denieth the Son, the same hath not the Father : [*but*] *he that acknowledgeth the Son hath the Father also.*

24 Let that therefore abide in you, which ye have heard from the beginning. If that which ye have heard from the beginning shall remain in you, ye also shall continue in the Son, and in the Father.

25 And this is the promise that he hath promised us, *even* eternal life.

26 These *things* have I written unto you concerning them that seduce you.

27 But the anointing which ye have received of him abideth in you, and ye need not that any man teach you : but as the same anointing teacheth you of all things, and is truth, and is no lie, and even as it hath taught you, ye shall abide in him.

28 And now, little children, abide in him ; that, when he shall appear, we may have confidence, and not be ashamed before him at his coming.

29 If ye know that he is righteous, ye know that every one that doeth righteousness is born of him.

SOME people have imagined that, on becoming a Christian, everything will be easy, and plain sailing, till they reach the Heavenly Harbour. Alas, in the disillusionment, and consequent reaction that follow, faith has had a rude shock. Yet a moment's reflection might have safeguarded them. Before their conversion, they were swimming down-stream, going with the tide, floating along on the current of popular opinion and practice ;   but now they have turned ("converted") and from that moment they have been swimming up-stream, against all that they, with the others, had formerly held and believed. Opposition, even antagonism, becomes their experience ; and they begin to realise that perils—some open, some hidden—lie in the Christian's path. Our passage deals with some of them, and hints at others. But let us go back, for consideration of the first of them, to the closing words of our last Study.

From Beneath

" *The wicked one* " (14). Don't be surprised that you have now attracted his attention. Time was when he did not bother you overmuch ; but all that has now changed. I have learnt something interesting about professional burglars. I am not talking about the petty breaking and entering, nor about the smash and grab merchant, but of the real thing. I have discovered that before he cracks a crib he makes it his business to find out all about the place first, and that he never carries out his plan unless he is pretty sure that there is something there worth taking. Our LORD says that the devil is " a murderer ", and that he is " a liar ", John viii. 44. May we venture to add that he is a burglar. Once he let you alone, for you had little worth his stealing ; but now that you have moved from your old house, " in Sin ", Colossians iii. 7, and have entered the new dwelling, " in Him ", Colossians i. 2, you have so much worth taking—a peace, a power, a joy, a reward, a blessing, a crown, Revelation iii. 11, which he would rob you of, if he can. Not that he cares very much about you and your loss. What he is out for is, through you, to hurt GOD—as he did with his then agent, Saul of Tarsus, who was injuring the Christians, and who heard the heavenly accusation, " Why persecutest thou *Me* ? " Acts ix. 4. By the way, ye Church members, forget not that he, or she, that touches one of the LORD's own, touches Him !

The devil is not omnipresent—since he is not GOD. It is not he personally that attacks and tempts every one of us. Naturally, he went in person to confront our LORD ; but in

the case of most of us he uses his varied agents—" the
devil, and his angels ", Matthew xxv. 41. If he is tempting
you, he can't be tempting me at the same time, for he cannot
be in two places at once. When he does himself appear, it is
often with strangely mixed characteristics—as a " serpent ",
Genesis iii. 1 ; as a " lion ", I Peter v. 8 ; even as " an angel
of light ", II Corinthians xi. 14. It is even possible for him
to use the Lord's own people, even the best of them, even an
apostle, as his tools—as when the Master so urgently chided
Peter, " Get thee behind Me, Satan ", Matthew xvi. 23. May
we never, never lend ourselves to his iniquitous designs by
leading any into sin ; by leading others astray into false
teachings that have no warrant of Holy Scripture ; or by
living inconsistent lives, to cause the enemies of the LORD to
blaspheme.

The devil is not omniscient—for neither does he share this
characteristic with Deity. Nevertheless, the range of his
knowledge seems to be quite unique. Judging by the variety
and subtlety of his temptations, he appears to possess a
wonderful acquaintance with human nature—playing, now
upon our weaknesses, now even upon our very strengths.
So that it is not for me to judge another man for his falls—
his temptations are not mine, any more than mine are his.
With knavish ingenuity, he knows how to bait his line for the
luring of us poor fish ! In all seriousness, let me point to
another example of what I would call his masterly intelligence
—in the realm of spiritism. The supposed appearances of
the beloved dead at seances are often fraudulent trickery ;
but by no means always so. The really sincere spiritualist
is more anxious than anyone to get rid of the fraud ; but
all the same I believe that he is unwittingly playing with
fire, in the face of such prohibitions as Leviticus xix. 31, and
Deuteronomy xviii. 11. I think there can be no question
that " appearances " of spirits do occur ; but I put it to all
interested that they are not the departed spirits of dear ones,
but evil spirits impersonating them. " Try the spirits ",
I John iv. 1 will presently say to us : mention to them the
name of JESUS, and see what will happen, verse 3. But how
is it that these " familiar spirits " are familiar with the little
tricks and oddities of the old friend that has been summoned
up ? I suggest that the *almost* omniscience of Satan is the
answer. We do not know what goes on in the mysterious

deeps of the Beneath world ; but we may not be far wrong if we hazard the guess that in that "wicked one's" army headquarters plans are made, and information is handed out, as the emissaries of evil go forth to enslave the minds and ruin the souls of men. No, not omniscient ; but he knows a rare lot !

The devil is not omnipotent—as GOD is. Strong he most certainly is; mighty, but not almighty. His power is far beyond anything that we ourselves can oppose to him. It is because of the fallacy that our pride entertains of our being a match for him in ourselves that we are so constantly defeated —but of that more anon. It is enough for the moment to recall, with uttermost thankfulness, that in the peril that comes to us from Beneath, we have at our call the "Stronger than the strong", Luke xi. 22, who will assuredly see us through to victory. Napoleon used to say, "Never underrate the power of the enemy", and he should know ! We have thought it well here to follow his advice.

FROM AROUND

"*The world*" (15-7). One of the members of the unholy trinity, a triumvirate of evil, set in array against the blessed Holy Trinity, to accomplish, if may be, our downfall. So we are now to consider another of the perils of the members of the Fellowship.

Its Nature—had better be clear in our minds. Whatever it prove to be, it is spoken of as an evil thing, so that we can at once rule out certain aspects of it: (*a*) *It is not the world of Matter*, as such—a form of false teaching at the basis of Gnosticism, a heresy which greatly troubled the early churches, e.g., the Colossian epistle. GOD could not have become incarnate because matter was innately evil. His only way of contact with the human world was through a descending gradation of æons. Of course, the Bible doctrine of the creation of the material world can have nothing to do with this abstruse and, as we should say, perverse teaching concerning our world. (*b*) *It is not the world of Nature*—true, this is not now what it once was in its pristine glory, for it bears grievous scars of the Fall of man, as Genesis iii. 17-8 said it would. Yet how filled with beautiful things and places it still remains. There is no evidence of its being inherently evil. (c) *It is not the world of Humanity*—as such, that is here alluded to, and that John iii. 16 refers to when it tells our wondering hearts that " GOD so loved the world ". (d) *It is all within the world that is alienate from God*—whether it be people, or things, or influences. Though it is a quite different avenue of temptation from that of the devil, he yet has a good deal to do with this also ; for, is he not, as the Master described him, " the prince of this world ", John xiv. 30, and referred to in another place as " the god of this world ", II Corinthians iv. 4, curious, even mysterious, utterances, but true as the Word is true.

Its Danger—the peril is not always recognised, so subtle is it. After all, what harm is there in doing this, going there, thinking that, saying the other ; and, while we dally, the harm is done. This verse makes plain that the world draws away our love from the Father : you can't have both. Many a Christian has found that profoundly true. He has seen no need for a life of separation from the world, and while discovering himself more and more embroiled in it, he has realised that his love for GOD, and for GOD's things, has been ebbing fast away—his old keenness for the Bible, the Prayer Meeting, the Worship, the Sunday has gone ; he is rapidly backsliding from grace. Sometimes, though with increasing rarity, a wistful mood is on him, and as he thinks back upon the simple happiness of those old days, he may ask himself, with Cowper,

> " Where is the blessedness I knew
> When first I saw the Lord ? "

Ah, we can tell him where it is—it has been thrown away into the world. Would GOD that he would return, and, in deepest penitence for his stupidity and sin, go on to say—

> " The dearest idol I have known,
> Whate'er that idol be.
> Help me to tear it from Thy throne
> And worship only Thee."

Do you recall Paul's poignant lament from prison, " Demas hath forsaken me, having loved this present world ", II Timothy iv. 10. What heartbreak such as he have, down the years, caused to those that loved them and hoped so much from them. I wonder what was the particular aspect of worldliness that was the lure of Demas ? John Bunyan, you remember, in " Pilgrim's Progress ", thought it was money—

the silver mine. How many erstwhile godly souls that has tripped and trapped !

Its Manifestations—there they are, set out for us in verse 16. (*a*) " The lust of the flesh "—evil desires emanating from the lower nature. What call is here for watchfulness in the realm of thought, " bringing into captivity every thought to the obedience of CHRIST ", II Corinthians x. 5—arresting, as like a policeman would, every unlawful intruder into the mind. (*b*) " The lust of the eyes "—evil desires entering through eye-gate. How many robbers of men's purity and peace have slipped in through that unguarded entrance. " When the woman saw . . ." Genesis iii. 6. " When I saw . . ." Joshua vii. 21. " When he saw . . ." I King xix. 3. 3. " When he saw . . ." Matthew xiv. 30. (*c*) " The pride of life "—" vain-glory " of life, as R.V. has it : evil desires arising out of the urge for wealth, position, comfort, power. Many a man has been brought down spiritually when he has climbed up materially. Money is not wrong, in itself ; but the love of money is : that, says I Timothy vi. 10, is—not, as A.V., the root of all evil, but " a root of every kind of evil ". Such, then, are the worldly characteristics, of which we must beware.

Its Duration—" the world passeth away " (17). It is not one of the eternal things. " We look not at the things which are seen, but at the things which are not seen : for the things which are seen are temporal, but the things which are not seen are eternal ", II Corinthians iv. 18. Gone will be the world, in the great earth catastrophe of II Peter iii. 10, and the believer, " abiding for ever ", will have been transported to a sphere where he will no longer be troubled by the " lust thereof ". Roll on, blessed day ! But we have not done with our perils yet—

FROM WITHIN

" The flesh " (16). We have already included a reference to this source of danger in our last section ; but we feel we must return to it, and take further, and deeper, cognizance of it. You see, it is one of the protagonists in the constant conflict in the arena of the soul. Look at Galatians v. 17—" The flesh lusteth against the SPIRIT, and the SPIRIT against the flesh . . . so that ye cannot do the thing that ye would "

The Christian at his new birth became a two-natured being, and the two are " contrary the one to the other ". The flesh is the old sinful nature, with which we were born, and which we inherited from Adam's fall, and which we retain till we get to the other side, when we shall lose it, as we shall also " the lust " of the world, to which we have just referred. The SPIRIT is the new nature, with which we are born again, the HOLY SPIRIT, Who Himself takes up His abode within the believer. John xiv. 17—all which we have elaborated in our second Study. It is the SPIRIT's warring that ensures the victory, so that " ye cannot [rather, need not] do the things [the wrong things] that ye [otherwise, without Him] would ". How gloriously optimistic does this make this verse, in contrast to the seeming pessimism of the A.V. But, let us not forget that in this " flesh "—and note that Paul does sometimes use the word in reference to the component of the human body, Galatians ii. 20—is the Christian's most insidious peril, against which we must be ever vigilant. That is a striking phrase in Siegfried Sassoon's poem which runs, " In me the tiger sniffs the rose ".

FROM ALONGSIDE

" *Antichrist* " (18)—the verse says that there are " many " such now, leading up to one outstanding evil personage at the close of the age. What has this not easy passage to tell us concerning this last of the perils that we have to beware of ?

Consider the presence of such—members of the Christian body for a time, they have now disclosed their true nature, and departed, to work their evil works upon the Church from outside. " They went out from us, but they were not of us " (19). Many a defaulter has been spoken of as a backslider when, in reality, they never had been Christians at all. Like those that Peter speaks of, " It is happened unto them according to the true proverb, The dog is turned to his own vomit again, and the sow that was washed to her wallowing in the mire ", II Peter ii. 22. They never were sheep, though they were thought to be. Now the veneer was off ; and in their reversion to type, they were seen to have been dogs and pigs all the time. A following of righteousness proves their new birth (29), a wallowing in unrighteousness shows they never were truly " new creatures ", II Corinthians v. 17.

Consider the meaning of such—the " anti " means not so much " opposed to ", but " instead of ". Westcott's illuminating comment is, the word " describes one who assuming the guise of CHRIST opposes CHRIST . . . the anti-christ assails CHRIST by proposing to do or to preserve what He did, while he denies Him ". The church of John's day had grave need to be warned of this danger ; while the church of our own day has equal need of the same. Movements and teaching professing to be Christian who yet " deny the Son " (23) some deny His Deity, some deny His miracles, some deny His virgin birth, some deny His word, some deny His atoning death, some deny His bodily resurrection, some deny His personal return. Anti-christs, the lot of them ! They preach another Christ than the One revealed in the New Testament—another Christ, which is not another, to adapt Paul's language about those who, similarly, preach " another gospel, which is not another ", Galatians i. 6–7. There is, can be, no other—there is but one Gospel, one CHRIST. When first we came to the study of this section, we thought it was concerned with a matter of vital importance for those early believers, but had little relevance to us ; but it has appeared, as we went along in our investigation, that " even now are there many antichrists " (18).

Consider the danger of such—" them that seduce you " (26). So often these people are individuals of such charming manners, obvious enthusiasm, delightful personality, high intellectuality, that they put you completely off your guard. Ponder some of the Christian Scientists, the Spiritualists, the Jehovah's Witnesses, that you have come across. How their courage and assiduity put us Christians to shame ! All the more seductive are they because they *seem*, only seem, to base their teaching on the Bible—in truth they " wrest the Scripture ", II Peter iii. 16, and so are ever " beguiling unstable souls ", II Peter ii. 14.

Consider the conquest of such—we come again to our glorious possession of the " Unction " (20). He, too, the great Teacher, in the face of false teaching, the great Safeguard, in the presence of dangerous doctrine, will take you, for your guidance, to the Holy Scriptures ; and, if you are willing to accept and obey His word, you shall be led aright, for " If any man will do [wills to do] His will, he shall know of the doctrine [the teaching], whether it be of GOD ", John vii. 17.

Such recognise the truth when they see it (21). We have spoken earlier of the Bible as the believer's Diet, making him strong. Here we find it as the Christian's Disinfectant, keeping him immune from all the " ism Diseases" floating around in the spiritual atmosphere alongside him. The same HOLY SPIRIT is spoken of also as the " Anointing " (27)—and the believer is assured that even if he is in a lone position, where there is not " any man " to whom he can turn for guidance, he shall yet find his way, because the SPIRIT will teach him independently of all human help. No man available ; but He is always at hand, for He " abideth in you ", never to be withdrawn. Yet He can, and will, be silenced, if we cease to " abide in Him " (28). This *abiding* of ours is *obeying* ; and so long as we continue to " do " the truth (not as in I John i. 6), we shall not only be in a position to know the truth here, but we shall " not be ashamed before Him at His coming ". Never to have answered His knock, never to have acknowledged His name, never to have engaged in His service, never to have reflected His character—then we may well be ashamed to meet Him ; but if, by an implicit reliance upon His HOLY SPIRIT, and a simple obedience to His Holy Will, we are carried through all our problems and perils, we may, in spite of our personal unworthiness, look forward with glad anticipation to Titus ii. 13's " [happy] Hope ". What a golden future awaits Fellowship members—

" As this old worn-out stuff, which is threadbare To-day
May become Everlasting To-morrow."

J. COLLINS.

Well may we adopt the words, though used in another sense, of George Meredith — " the rapture of the forward view."

VI

THE PORTRAITS OF THE FELLOWSHIP

I JOHN iii. 1-3

1 Behold, what manner of love the Father hath bestowed upon us, that we should be called the sons of God : therefore the world knoweth us not, because it knew him not.

2 Beloved, now are we the sons of God, and it doth not yet appear what we shall be : but we know that, when he shall appear, we shall be like him ; for we shall see him as he is.

3 And every man that hath this hope in him purifieth himself, even as he is pure.

MOST of the scholars are agreed that the two main sections and subjects of this Epistle are—(a) i–ii : Light ; (b) iii–v : Love. Which being so, we shall find the prevailing emphasis of these three chapters is on this second Attribute of GOD, and Requirement of His people. It is striking to note that within the compass of these sixty-six verses, the Noun occurs sixteen times, the Adjective five times, the Verb twenty-five times. Love is indeed the theme ; and as love is so strangely violated by so many in the Fellowship, this portion of the Word may carry much blessing as we study it together. I hope I shall not be held too facile, or too fanciful, in suggesting that these present verses give us an essay in Christian portraiture. It is one resemblance that we see, taken from three angles.

THE FAMILY LIKENESS

" Behold, what manner of love the Father hath bestowed upon us, that we should be called the sons of GOD " (1). GOD doesn't call every man a son of GOD, though some men do. His statement, through Paul, exclusively to believers, is, " Ye are all the children of GOD by faith in CHRIST JESUS ", Galatians iii. 26. Or, as our Epistoller says, writing as Gospeller, " As many as received Him, to them gave He power to become the sons of GOD, even to them that believe on His Name ", John i. 12. So, reader, and writer, are we, by this token, really children of GOD ? Then, think of—

The amazing love—" what manner of love ". Not for any worthiness, or attractiveness, of our own, seeing that it was " when we were without strength (helpless to save ourselves) . . . while we were yet sinners (repellent to holiness) . . . when were enemies (actually antagonistic to His grace) ", Romans v. 6, 8, 10, that GOD set His love upon us. That is a remarkable word that is translated, " what manner of ". They tell me that its root significance is not so much of what kind, but of what country, which the learned Dr. Vincent confirms. What an impressive effect that has on the other passages where it is found—for instance (a) " What manner of Man is this, that even the winds and the sea obey Him " Matthew viii. 27—of what country : not an earthly, seeing He has such authority, surely He belongs to another clime. (b) " This Man, if He were a prophet, would have known what manner of woman this is that toucheth Him : for she is a sinner ", Luke vii. 39—of what country : in their self-righteous superiority, they would not allow her to claim fellow-citizenship with themselves ; surely she belongs to some nether region, beneath their recognition. (c) " Seeing that all these things shall be, what manner of persons ought ye to be ", II Peter iii. 11—of what country : a land beyond the skies, we are as pilgrims, travelling thitherward through the alien country of this present world. And now (d) " What manner of love the Father has bestowed upon us ", verse 1— of what country : no earthly kingdom contains, nor could cultivate a love of such sweet quality as this : only the dews and breezes of the Heavenly expanses could ever produce so bountiful, and so beautiful, a harvest.

The established relationship—" that we should be called the sons of GOD ". What a privilege is this, to be numbered amongst the elect, and select, people of God, to be incorporated into the eternal Family of the Most High, to be grafted into the blessed Fellowship of CHRIST and His Church. It is well to be reminded that Family, and Fellowship go together. There are special difficulties arising from being an only child in a family, which problems frequently arise in the case of those who fail to recognise that while we are " born again " one by one, we are not saved to live and serve in isolation, but in community. To be brought into the family of His children is to be brought, at the same time, into the fellowship of His Church. Let us make much of our church membership, and seek to avoid, where possible, the spirit of free-lance Christianity. You remember the story of the old lady who, watching her son's regiment march by, exclaimed, " Look ! our Tom's the only one in step ! " Beware of that attitude in spiritual things. It is one of the dangers of rigid, and rabid denomi-nationalism. How we thank GOD, then, for our Divinely granted relationship with Himself, and with our fellow Christians.

The expected resemblance—The children should bear some resemblance to the Heavenly Father. " Walk in love, as CHRIST also hath loved us ", Ephesians v. 2 ; " Be ye holy, for I am holy ", I Peter i. 16 ; " Be ye therefore perfect, even as your Father which is in heaven is perfect ", Matthew v. 48. Even the people of the world expect professing Christians to be a little Christ-like, and accuse us of the lack of it. Do you observe a hint of that in the last clause of this first verse ? " Therefore the world knoweth us not, because it knew Him not." Put that round the other way, and say that if the world knew Him, it would recognise the likeness in us. Here is a boy I know, who has very distinctive features, who one day introduces me to his father—then I discover where he gets that mouth from, that colouring, that nose, etc. Like father, like son ! It is a solemn, and salutory, question for each believer to ask himself : How far am I like Him ? There is another form of portraiture for us now to consider, what I would venture to call—

THE PHOTOGRAPHIC LIKENESS

" *Beloved, now are we the sons of God, and it doth not yet appear what we shall be : but we know that, when He shall appear, we shall be like Him, for we shall see Him as He is* " (2) Beloved : the apostle uses the greeting in no formal way : others may employ the word in a quite perfunctory manner, but not he. This man with a heart full of love embraced all in a feeling of real affection. Some time ago I was staying with Bishop J. H. Linton, and during those few days, he said, more than once, a simple little thing that greatly impressed me—" You know, I love *people* ". You could

see he did ; you could see John did. I think the Bishop's
" J " ought to be John, but alas, it isn't ! Well now, what
about this photographic likeness, which the apostle longed to
see reproduced in these that he so loved. What is required
in order to get it ?

A Prepared Plate—" Now are we the sons of GOD ". Only
so are we properly prepared, and susceptible to the reception
of the image. In an ordinary photograph, it is no good
expecting anything from any untreated piece of glass—it
must be scientifically got ready for its special purpose. The
spiritual preparation is covered by that part of our second
verse that we have quoted at the opening of this paragraph—
" now we are the sons of GOD ". *No delay*—" now ". We
haven't to wait till the end : we are now the possessors, the
inheritors, of this amazing privilege. *No doubt*—" are ".
There is no perhaps, or maybe, about it. We do not just
think, or merely hope, we know we are. John wrote his
Gospel in order that " ye might *have* life ", John xx. 31. He
wrote this Epistle in order that " ye may *know* that ye have
eternal life ", I John v. 13. Some people say that it is very
presumptuous to speak with such certainty; but—which is
the more presumptuous, to believe GOD's word, or to doubt
it ? *No difference*—" We ". Every real Christian can believe
it, whatever little progress in the SPIRIT he may have made,
however little knowledge of GOD he may have gained. " We "
Christians—old and young, wise and foolish, important and
insignificant, all of us, because it is not of our merit, or achieve-
ment, but entirely of His grace, can count it true that " now
are we . . ."

That, then, is the all-over covering of the plate of our
being, that makes us ready to bear the likeness. But let us
analytically examine the spiritual chemistry here, and see
what are the component elements that make up this receptive
quality. I think they are mainly three (*a*) *We are born again*—
so that our very nature is completely changed ; so that we
are no longer, as it were, ordinary glass. (*b*) *We are washed in
the Blood*—so that our very hearts are cleansed from the
defilement of sin. (*c*) *We are indwelt by the Spirit*—so that
our very lives are possessed by the power for holiness. These
are the blessed ingredients which are included within this
potent preparation of the plate for Divine portraiture, our
being " sons of GOD ". Now for the next step—

A Momentary Look—" We shall see Him as He is ". We spoke earlier of the damage that one look can do to the soul ; but here is a quite different result of just one look, effecting immortal transformation in the soul. I have seen some lovely sights in my time—a distant view of the rolling hills about the Devil's Dyke in the downs behind Brighton ; the sight of a J. C. Gibbs racing for the line at Twickenham to touch the rugger ball down behind the goal posts, quickening a sportsman's pulse to race with him ; a look at the immaculate cricketer, Jack Hobbs, executing with such precision that mighty sweep to leg which used so often to open his innings ; a ravishing observation through a powerful microscope of one of nature's tiny marvels—the exquisite beauty and order of a snow-flake, or an insect's wing ; the look through William Wordsworth's eyes at a hundred beauties and wonders of land and sky—about Keswick country, and beyond ; the moving sight of a great congregation rapt to catch every syllable of the preacher's message. Many such sights, and many more, have stirred my heart. But—but—I am going to see presently one sight that will eclipse them all : " we shall see Him ! " What an indescribably lovely thing that first sight of Him is going to be. What a purifying impression it is going to make. Some folks tell us—how strange that the Bible doesn't mention it—that the fires of purgatory are needful to make us fit for the holy presence of GOD ; but those who come unbiased to this verse of the Epistle will discover that one look, one momentary look, at Him will be gloriously sufficient to transfigure the least and the lowest into a perfect presentment of the Saviour. The lens of the camera takes a momentary look, its plate has been duly prepared for the occasion, and lo—

An Instantaneous Impression—" We shall be like Him ". If you know anything about your own " deceitful " heart, Jeremiah xvii. 9, you will acknowledge this to be one of the outstanding marvels of His Advent appearance, that you (yes, you), and I (yes, I) are to be, in a moment, changed into the perfect likeness of CHRIST. Is this really feasible ? It was as if the HOLY SPIRIT, Who inspired John to write, knew that you would find this difficult to believe, and so led him to put this thing up against the things we don't know. " It doth not yet appear what we shall be "—what sort of resurrection body shall we have ; what degree of memory shall we carry over into the next life ; how shall we recognise there, in their transfigured form, those whom we have loved down here. It is not for our good that we should know these things, and many others, or they would have been revealed. But, says John, in effect, I'll tell you what we may be certain about. Lots of things about the future we don't know ; but two things we do know. (*a*) "*He shall appear*"—in spite of all the wishful thinking of the sinner, in spite of all the unbelief of many a teacher, in spite of all the ridicule of the impious, in spite of all the disregard of the pre-occupied, He shall appear : oh, glorious day ! (*b*) "*We shall be like Him*"—we find it hard to accept, as we have said. Too good to be true, we have felt. Put all that aside, as unworthy of one who should be accepting all that He said as right, rest your soul on this His unbreakable, unshakable, promise, and, with a gay heart, look forward to the miracle. One sight of Him, and the photograph is taken. Ay, but we are not there yet : what shall we do meanwhile ?

The Artistic Likeness

"*Every man that hath this hope in him purifieth himself, even as He is pure*" (3). The artist, in order to secure his picture, works so differently from the photographer. He has his model, he paints or chips patiently away, until he is able at last to present his finished study. There is nothing of quick accomplishment for him, but a going on, and going on. So it is here with our third photogravure in mind ; and, once again, three things contribute to its success.

The Big Incentive—"Every man that hath this hope in him ". This hope of His Return. How strangely mistaken are these people who suppose that the Advent Hope has no practical value for decent living, and encourages idle stargazing. Observe any Christian man or woman who really believes in the Second Coming, and I venture to say you will find in either of them holiness of life and busyness of service. The thought of meeting Him is one of the biggest incentives of the spiritual life, with its constant reminder, " Be ye also ready ", Matthew xxiv. 44. Look at the word " hope " for a moment. In the New Testament it always means a certainty. It is not, " I have not got it, but I hope I may ", but " I have not yet got it, but I know I shall ", that is certain. The approaching Advent is a sure thing. He might also notice the little word, " in ", which could be more happily translated " upon ", followed by a capital " H ". The A.V. looks as if the phrase means that the man has his hope within him, in his own heart ; but the real meaning is quite different, and runs this way, " every man that hath this Hope set upon Him ". The hope is not, in any sense, resting upon ourselves ; but upon the unchangeable CHRIST. It is that which gives it the certainty that it assuredly possesses. And now we see that to hold this truth of His Return is to impart to life a great desire, and decision, to endeavour to represent Him now in our character and conduct. For now, in this artist's attempt, we have—

The Perfect Model—" even as He is pure ". What a perfect, and, if left to our own resources, what an impossible Model to copy. Yet, as we learn from I Peter i. 21, CHRIST has left us " an Example, that ye should follow His steps ". It has often been pointed out that the word here translated " example " is the word for a " copy-head ". My older readers will remember the old days [" the good old days " ?] when we were taught how to write by those means. An automatically inscribed adage was at the head of the page—" A Stitch in Time saves Nine ", " A Bird in the Hand is worth Two in the Bush ", etc. —and we had to copy it line by line down the page. It was always noticeable that our effort deteriorated as we got farther away from the headline. Such is the picture Peter employs, with the impressive lesson, that if we would make a decent copy we must take care to keep close up to the Head. Of the man who wrote these very words we read, " But Peter followed Him afar off ", Matthew xxvi. 58—he followed, but far off ; that's why he made such a mess of his copy-book ! Let no distance separate between you and Him—nothing of sin, to blot the page ; nothing of self, to spoil the script of your behaviour ; nothing between, to diminish your resemblance to Him, in the holiness of your life, in the happiness of your soul, in the helpfulness of your actions.

> " Let it be seen that with Thee I have been,
>   JESUS, my Lord and my Saviour.
> Let it be known I am wholly Thine own,
>   By all my speech and behaviour."

That leads us on to consider—

The Growing Portrait—" purifieth himself ". But I thought

it was He, not we, that did the purifying work. Yes, you are quite right. Why, then, " purifieth *himself* " ? See that piece of soap ? That is a rare purifier : but only if you take the trouble to use it. Then you will say that you washed yourself. Yet really it was the soap : you only wash yourself when you use the means provided. Just so is it with the purification of this verse. The HOLY SPIRIT is the Divinely provided Means—*He* does it. Our part is to use the way that GOD supplies—in that sense, *we* do it. Look at II Corinthians iii, 18—" We all, with open face [nothing between us and Him] beholding as in a glass [the mirror of the Word] the glory of the Lord, are changed into the same image from glory to glory, even as by the Lord the SPIRIT ". You see again it is, primarily and fundamentally, He that does it. We do it only by employing the cleansing agent of the Word, as our Lord Himself says, in John xv. 3, " Now ye are clean through the Word which I have spoken unto you " ; and as our very Epistle has told us, i. 7, " the Blood of JESUS cleanseth ". Notice once more " cleanseth ", a present tense, " purifieth ", same tense—it is a continuing thing. To return to our illustration of the portraits, this is the gradual appearance, day by day, of the likeness—" from glory to glory ". Expecting to " see the King in His beauty ", Isaiah xxxiii. 17, how anxious we shall be to keep clean, to grow increasingly like Him. Wouldn't you be ashamed if, on being commanded to a Royal Audience at Buckingham Palace, you found that you had got splashed with mud on the way. So does James i. 27 warn us that part of " pure religion and undefiled before GOD and the Father is this . . . to keep himself unspotted from the world ". Well now, to recapitulate, if we are sons and daughters of GOD, we are expected to exhibit something of the Family Likeness ; one day we shall be transformed into His perfect likeness to Him, even in the conditions of this world, and in the circumstances of our own personal environment, " more holiness give me, more likeness to Thee ", as the hymn says. So—what sort of a portrait are we ? On visiting a friend's house, we have sometimes gone into the drawing-room, and picking up a photograph from the mantelpiece, have said, " Who's this ? " And we have been chided for not knowing, " It's so and so ". " Why, I shouldn't have known him." Another occasion, we have taken up a photograph and exclaimed, " Isn't that exactly like him ? " Tell me, what sort

of a portrait are we of Him ? " May others see JESUS in me ",
we sing. Well, do they ?

A missionary was telling the story of JESUS—how kind He
was, how gentle, how good, when a little heathen child said,
" Please, that man used to live here ". Of course she was
mistaken ; but, you see, some while before a man lived in her
village, so kind, so gentle, so good, that the child, when she
heard about JESUS, thought at once that that must have been
He. What a testimony to him ! What a portrait of Him !

VII

THE PURITY OF THE FELLOWSHIP

I JOHN iii. 4–9

4 Whosoever committeth sin transgresseth also the law : for sin is the transgression of the law.

5 And ye know that he was manifested to take away our sins : and in him is no sin.

6 Whosoever abideth in him sinneth not : whosoever sinneth hath not seen him, neither known him.

7 Little children, let no man deceive you : he that doeth righteousness is righteous, even as he is righteous.

8 He that committeth sin is of the devil ; for the devil sinneth from the beginning. For this purpose the Son of God was manifested, that he might destroy the works of the devil.

9 Whosoever is born of God doth not commit sin ; for his seed remaineth in him ; and he cannot sin, because he is born of God.

FOR all the emphasis of this second part of the Epistle upon the subject of love, it can't avoid tackling the subject of Sin, the very negation of love. Over and over again, throughout the Letter, the matter crops up—either in its negative aspect of sin, or in its positive aspect of holiness. Our present passage takes up this positive side, and discusses for us the whole question of purity of living for the believer. For the believer, notice ; because the verses and truths are not for the non-Christian. The very words will be as a foreign language to him, but the real Christian, though he may not understand it all, will be able gratefully to enter into much of it. So he finds his purity—

AS PROVIDED IN THE LORD

The standard set—is the point of verse 4, " the law ". However you may define or interpret that word, I think you will not be far wrong if you regard it as GOD's ideal, GOD's will, for His people. There it was, set up for His people Israel at Sinai, when first they were welded into nationhood, this was the covenant law of their Theocratic kingdom, Exodus xx. 18. And now, away on into the New Testament, here is a keen young man, who comes to ask the Master, " What shall I do that I may inherit eternal life ? " Mark x. 17. For answer our LORD sets up before him the same law as He said elsewhere, " This do and thou shalt live ", Luke x. 28. And if we want to know the inner meaning and clear summing up of the law, we have only to listen again to the Master, as He interprets the " Thou shalt ", and " Thou shalt not ", by " Thou shall love ". Taking up the two sections of the commandments, He shows the way that to keep the first four, Our Duty towards God, is, " Thou shalt love the Lord . . . with all thy heart, soul, mind ", and the observing of the last six, Our Duty towards our neighbour, is in the injunction, " Thou shalt love thy neighbour as thyself ", Matthew xxii. 36–9. " On these two commandments hang all the law and the prophets ". There it is, " the law ".

Unfortunately, the people of the world are sitting more and more loosely these days to the Ten Commandments. They want none such. " Why can't we do as we like ? " they ask restively and rebelliously. May GOD preserve us from all such throwing off of moral and spiritual restraint that keeps us sane and sober, " Where there is no vision the people cast off restraint, Proverbs xxix. 18, R.V. More adulteries, more divorces, more suicides, more murders, more scandals—do as we like ? No, thank you. Rather we pray, " GOD save the people ! "

Ah, but some will remind me of Romans vi. 14, " Ye are not under the law, but under grace ". So what ? Does that mean that I need no longer heed the law ? Paul himself, in the next verse, asks the very question, and energetically repudiates the suggestion—" Shall we sin ? . . . GOD forbid ". The very conception of sin, in this verse, is that it is an exhibition of a dispensing with law—" whosoever committeth sin doeth law-lessness " (R.V.). It is the violation of the law of our being, the law which includes our threefold relation, to GOD, to others, and to ourselves, as Westcott put it. Surely, the point of the Romans statement is, not that we have no further obligation to keep the law, but that we have now a new incentive to keep it. Law tells me that here is something that I *ought* to do ; grace is that which so fills my heart that I *want to* do it. Law is Love's gift ; Love is Law's keeping— that says the Lord, in His Word, and in my heart, is the way grace revolutionises the whole matter. With what ecstasy

does the Psalmist exclaim, " O how I love Thy law . . .",
Psalm cxix. 97. And now comes the uncomfortable reflection,
" But, you know, you haven't kept it ! "

We are forced to acknowledge ourselves " guilty " before
GOD, Romans iii. 19. And that is one of the three gracious
purposes of the Law, which lie behind that great saying of
Galatians iii. 24, " the law was our schoolmaster to bring us
unto CHRIST ". Three great lessons it taught us, (1) We ought,
(2) We haven't, (3) We can't. So our very helplessness drives
us to CHRIST, who alone has Himself kept the law, and who
alone can put us fully right (" righteous ") with the law—
" that we might be justified by faith ", as the Galatians' word
continues. How ready we are, then, to be brought unto
CHRIST, in Whom we find—

The failure met—" He was manifested " (5, 8) for that very
purpose. Long " before the foundation of the world ",
I Peter i. 20—before there was a world, before there was a
race, before there was a sin, GOD knew what would happen,
and what would be the unhappy plight of the men that should
be, and in the Council Chamber of Deity a plan of salvation
was drawn up to meet the situation that would arise. And
now, in process of time, appeared the Divine Executant of the
Plan of Grace. This was the prime cause of His being " manifested " among men. He did other things incidentally—
shewing us the Father, John xiv. 7 ; leaving as an Example,
I Peter ii. 21 ; and so on. But the fundamental reason for
His becoming Man was, as I Timothy i. 15 so clearly teaches
us, " This is a faithful saying, and worthy of all acceptation,
[This is a true story !] that CHRIST JESUS came into the world
to save sinners . . .". Or, again, " The Son of Man is come to
seek, and to save that which was lost ", Luke xix. 10. And
how did He do it ? Verse 5 hints at the answer.

" *To take away our sins* "—His precious Blood is the
Sovereign Eraser of all our guilty stain. The blood of the
Old Testament sacrifices could not do that—" It is not possible
that the blood of bulls and of goats should *take away* sins ",
Hebrews x. 4 : could not remove them, but only cover them.
That is what the root of the word " atonement " really
signifies. Strangely enough, it is the word that is translated
" pitch " in Genesis vi. 14, and is used of the ark's covering,
thou " shalt pitch it within and without with pitch ". It is an
Old Testament idea ; and the word does not properly occur

in the New Testament—the one exception is in Romans v. 11, and even there R.V. changes " atonement " to " reconciliation ". The word, then, means covering, and the fact effects reconciliation. Old Testament believers were covered by the blood of their sacrifices, until the time for the shedding of the Blood of the One Eternal Sacrifice, which should " take away " their sins. Is that not what Romans iii. 25 means, " Whom GOD hath set forth to be a propitiation through faith in His Blood, to declare His righteousness for the remission of *sins that are past*, through the forbearance of GOD "—that is, I think, sins of past ages, or, again, Hebrews ix. 15, " He is the mediator of the new testament that, by means of death, for the redemption of the *transgressions that were under the first testament* . . ." ; there it is again. His death, His Blood, were retrospective in effect. Calvary has no date. Abraham, Moses, and the rest, will be in heaven with you, and for the same reason, " the Blood of JESUS CHRIST "—shed in grace, and love, " to take away our sins ".

" *In Him is no sin* "—that was more than just a fact : it was one of the fundamental necessities of the whole transaction. As we saw in an earlier Study, " the Lamb of GOD " is the fulfilment of the lambs of old ; and as they must be certified to be stainless, " without blemish ", Exodus xii. 5, so He must be declared to be sinless, " I find no fault in Him ", John xix. 4. If He had sin of His own, He must die for Himself, and could not be justifiably eligible to die for others. Thank GOD, *in* Him is no sin ; but *on* Him was all sin, Isaiah liii. 6. At the pivotal point of the world's redemption, GOD brought all the sin that ever was, and laid it upon Him ; and GOD brought all the sin that ever shall be, and laid that also upon Him— " laid ", made to meet on Him the iniquity of us all.

" *That He might destroy the works of the devil* "—here is a second purpose for which " the Son of GOD was manifested ", here among men. This is one of the reasons for Deity taking Humanity. " He that committeth sin is of the devil "—St. Augustine's comment was, " The devil made no one, he begot no one, he created no one ; but whosoever imitates the devil [*i.e.*, by doing sin, as he does] is, as it were, a child of the devil, through imitating, not through being born of him ". Did not our Lord JESUS say the same thing, when, addressing His enemies, He declared, " ye are of your father the devil, and the lusts of your father ye will do ", John viii. 44. The

Master, then, made it His aim to " destroy the works of the
devil "—I am greatly tempted to paraphrase " the works ",
and call it " the workings ".   The scholars may not allow that
as a translation : I only offer it as a rendering of what seems
to me to be the intention of the word.   But look at that other
word, " destroy ".   Is it to be understood as referring to that
yet distant day when " the devil and his angels ", " the devil
and all his works ", shall be utterly done away ? Revelation
xx. 10.   Thank GOD for that coming Day of Final Triumph ;
but has the word some relevance for us here and now ?   Is
there any sense in which He may be said to " destroy " his
works in the present ?   There is another New Testament
passage in which the word occurs which, in my own view,
justifies us in giving the word the meaning " render void ",
" make inoperative ", almost " draw the sting ".   Examine it,
then, in that other passage, Romans vi. 6, " Knowing this,
that our old man [the man of old ; the man we used to be—
Evan Hopkins] is crucified with Him, that the body of sin
[the body as the medium of sin] might be *destroyed*, that
henceforth we should not serve sin ".   It is evident, isn't it,
that the body is not literally destroyed ; but it is part of
GOD's plan for us that the body be " loosed " (the Greek word
translated " destroyed ") from its tendency to serve as sin's
instrument, Romans vi. 13.   Transfer that now to our Epistle,
and I think you have its true significance. It is one of the
beneficent results of His Cross that, for those who take advan-
tage of it, He has drawn the sting from all the workings of
Satan, and that, however he may fulminate, or fascinate, he
is powerless to affect the believer, unless we are so foolish as
to yield to his persuasions.   At Golgotha was fought the greatest
battle of the ages, and the devil was completely conquered.
He remains our bitter foe ; but he is a beaten foe—never
forget that.   After the abolition of slavery there were many
Negroes who were unaware that freedom had been won for
them, and who consequently still suffered from, in many
cases, cruel bondage : their masters knew all right, but their
slaves didn't—and so they were exploited.   As is many a
Christian, untaught in this great truth, exploited by his most
cunning slave driver.   The act of emancipation has been
promulgated ; but if we, through ignorance, indolence, or
inadvertence, fail to act upon it, Satan, quite aware of the
true position, is diabolically clever enough to keep us " tied

and bound with the chain of our sins ". So has our gracious
GOD provided, " in CHRIST ", for the believer's purity. Now
let us see that—

AS PRACTICED IN THE CHRISTIAN

Here, in verses 6–7, we see the beginnings of the high
doctrine that John has preached being worked out in practice.
In the first of the two verses we have two Present Tenses
that are of exceeding importance in the Christian life. (1)
" *Abideth* "—the New Testament attaches such value to this
abiding that it would obviously be to our great profit to try
to discover what is its actual significance. It is one of the
big secrets of abounding fruit, " He that abideth in Me, and
I in him, the same bringeth forth much fruit," John xv. 5.
" Abiding is abounding," as the late beloved, epigrammatic,
Bishop Taylor Smith used to say. It is one of the big secrets
of effectual prayer, " If ye abide in Me, and My words abide
in you, ye shall ask what ye will, and it shall be done unto
you," John xv. 7. Both specific undertakings on the part of
the covenant Lord, which He will, without fail, bring to
pass, provided that we, on our part, fulfil the condition :
" abideth ". And now we have it again in John's Letter, as
one of the big secrets of a holy life, " Whosoever abideth in
Him sinneth not ". Ah, yes, we simply must try to find out
what it means—and I am going to suggest something very
matter-of-fact, something common or garden. When I was
looking into the subject, I was greatly struck with those words
of the Master in John xv. 10, " If ye keep My commandments,
ye shall abide in My love "—as if obeying were abiding !
Anyhow, if they are not to be thought to be synonymous terms,
at least it may safely be assumed that the one is, from one
angle, the sign, and, from another angle, the sequel, of the
other. Are you abiding ? You are not sure ? Well, are you
obeying ? Yes ? Then, you are abiding. Let us eschew the
seeking for some metaphysical, emotional, mystical explanation ; but, rather, apply this simple test. I think we shall
be not far wrong.

Look now at our second Present Tense. (2) " *Sinneth not* "
—the tense of the Greek verb satisfies us that the meaning is
not, committeth not an occasional act of sin, but continueth
not in an habitual practice of sin. The former is, alas, not

uncommon even in Christians—we do commit acts of sin ; and this apostle has made allowance and provision for that fact when, in ii. 1, he wrote, " If any man sin . . .". But the point here is different : it is, a life of sinning. An act of sin, in a believer, is serious enough ; but a life of sin is immeasurably blameworthy. Of course, a life of plain, simple, day-by-day, step-by-step obedience would safeguard any Christian from any such presumption ; while a continuance in that sordid way should cause him to question whether he had actually ever " seen " or " known " Him personally for himself.

We come on, in verse 7, to another of our Present Tenses— " *Doeth righteousness* "—we have left the negative, and are now at the positive. Everyone acquainted with the New Testament epistles is aware of the distinction between imputed and imparted righteousness. The moment we believe, our sins are cleansed through His precious Blood, and our souls are clothed with His spotless Righteousness. This is the sense of the word, for instance, in 1 Corinthians i. 30, " Ye are in CHRIST JESUS, who of GOD is made unto us . . . righteousness ". We are reckoned as righteous—because we are now, no longer, " in sin ", but " in CHRIST ". But then comes the necessity to live a righteous life. Even as in Romans i. 7 and I Corinthians i. 2, R.V., says we are " called saints ", while A.V. says we are " called *to be* saints ". There is, as you are aware, no " to be " in the original—but how right both Versions are. We are called to be what we are. Reckoned as righteous, our life has consistently to correspond thereto— we are to " do righteousness ". Let no man trade on his standing before GOD, in imputed righteousness ; but let him earnestly look to his state before men, by the imparting of the HOLY SPIRIT, even as the LORD was ever righteous, not only in innate nature, but in His daily walk with men. Be not deceived into imagining that, while conversion is of importance, conduct doesn't matter—you'll get there in the end ! Will you ? And now, in verse 9, we go on to consider Christian purity—

AS PERFECTED IN THE BEHAVIOUR

This is one of the most difficult portions in all the New Testament ; but here it is in the course of our expositional enquiry, so we must not shirk or shelve it. After all, it is part of the Word of GOD, and it is written for our learning. It has a meaning for us, a message for us, so that we must now humbly try to find out what was the SPIRIT'S purpose in leading John to write such words.. I offer three reflections upon the verse :

It States a Fact—" born of GOD ". This describes every reader to whom the Epistle was addressed : birth is the beginning of life, new birth is the beginning of the new life. How surprised Nicodemus was when our Lord said to him, " Ye must be born again ". That was understandable for a man in the gutter of sin ; but he was not that sort—brought up in a godly home ; early taught the Old Scriptures ; growing to be an office-bearer in the church ; and now the leading Bible expositor of his day—" *the* [R.V.] master in Israel ". Yet, in spite of all this, our Lord tells him that, to all intents and purposes, he had not begun—" ye must be born again ". It isn't only the bad people, but the good people as well, who " must " : *you* " must ". Is this great, eternal fact a fact in your own personal experience ? You see, the members of the Fellowship are not only Servants, Soldiers, Subjects, but Sons. The simplest explanation of how this comes about is, I think, in John i. 12—" To as many as received Him, to them gave He power to become the sons of GOD, even to them that believe on His Name ". When we do, for ourselves personally, receive the Lord JESUS into our hearts and lives as our own Saviour and Lord, that moment we are given this mysterious, life-changing " power " of new birth. How vividly some Christians can recall the day, and the circumstances, when it happened ; how sadly others regret that they cannot put their finger on any precise moment. I fancy it was for the comfort of these latter that the closing words of our new-birth verse were added—" even to them that believe on His Name ". You don't personally know your physical birthday—you've been told, and you have taken it for granted ; but, date or no date, you know you are alive ! Even so, although you do not know the date of your new birth, you do " believe "—which proves that you really are a child of GOD. The blessed fact is *your* fact.

It Shows an Effect—" He cannot sin ". But writing to the same group of people he said, " If any man sin ", ii. 1, as if he can ! Once again the explanation lies in the use of the

tenses. The " if " clause is in the aorist, and means to commit
an act of sin—which even a Christian can do. This clause is
in the present, and means to continue in a life of sin—which
a Christian cannot do. Verse 6 said he does not ; this verse 9
says he cannot. Apart from the possibility of an occasional
stumble along the way, the main trend of his journey is, all
the while, in purity and holiness. But, of course, that " cannot sin " is a claim of so sweeping a nature that we seek for
some justification for it ; and our verse does not fail us.

It Suggests a Secret—" His seed remaineth in him ". We
shall have additional remarks to make when we come to
chapter v. 18 ; and for the moment we confine ourselves to
what is said here. Well, then, " His seed "—that is, GOD's
seed—" remaineth in him ". Note I Peter i. 23, " Being born
again, not of corruptible seed, but of incorruptible. . . ."
This new Seed, new Life, new Nature, abides in him, and
therein lies his secret against sin. You have the same thought
of the two natures remaining within the believer in Galatians
v. 17, " the flesh . . . and the SPIRIT . . .", as we considered
earlier. The " born of GOD " people are thus two-natured
persons ; and it is the new-nature, the new " I ", of Galatians
ii. 20, that " cannot sin ". Do you recall that strange word
of Paul's in Romans vii. 20, " Now if I do that I would not,
it is no more I that do it, but sin that dwelleth in me ".
When any sin eventuates, it is the old nature, the flesh that
does it ; the new nature, the now real new " I ", " cannot
sin ". Of course, this is given to us only as an explanation,
not as an excuse—there is no reason why it should happen.
A rubber ball cannot sink—unless it is held down. We must
not let our old, sinful nature get us down ! There we will
defer the matter, until we take it up later in that further
verse I mentioned just now.

So does our Heavenly Father make due provision for the
purity of His sons and daughters, leaving us without excuse
if we fall into unclean ways.

VIII

THE PRACTICALITY OF THE FELLOWSHIP

I JOHN iii. 10–18

10 In this the children of God are manifest, and the children of the devil : whosoever doeth not righteousness is not of God, neither he that loveth not his brother.

11 For this is the message that ye heard from the beginning, that we should love one another.

12 Not as Cain, *who* was of that wicked one, and slew his brother. And wherefore slew he him ? Because his own works were evil, and his brother's righteous.

13 Marvel not, my brethren, if the world hate you.

14 We know that we have passed from death unto life, because we love the brethren. He that loveth not *his* brother abideth in death.

15 Whosoever hateth his brother is a murderer ; and ye know that no murderer hath eternal life abiding in him.

16 Hereby perceive we the love *of God*, because he laid down his life for us : and we ought to lay down *our* lives for the brethren.

17 But whoso hath this world's good, and seeth his brother have need, and shutteth up his bowels *of compassion* from him, how dwelleth the love of God in him ?

18 My little children, let us not love in word, neither in tongue ; but in deed and in truth.

CHRISTIANITY is so intensely practical. It never allows us to forget that if it does not " work " it is spurious. " Faith without works is dead," James ii. 26. Not that works are the cause of salvation, but they are the consequence of it, as Paul is led to tell us, in a classic passage, " Saved . . . not of works . . . *unto* good works," Ephesians ii. 8–10. At the end of his birthday a small boy was a-bed when an uncle came in with a belated present—a clockwork engine. How pleased was the little fellow, and how eager for the morning, when he could see how it worked ! That is one of the special blessings of Monday Morning—Sunday has brought you some special blessing, and next day is your first chance to see that it works. " Shew forth His salvation from [Mon-] day to [Satur-] day ", says Psalm xcvi. 2. " Work out your own salvation ", says Philippians ii. 12—" your own ", because you received it from Him, and now, by His indwelling, He enables you to work it out in practice.

In the section before us, Paul takes up certain subjects which he has already dealt with—righteousness, love, sacrifice, kindness. Only now, he treats them, not theoretically, not emotionally, not doctrinally—but practically. I remind you of what we saw in i. 6, where our apostle speaks of those who " *do* not the truth ". You see, truth is not merely something to be believed, something to be preached, but something to be *done*. All doctrine ends in doing. On, then, to our verses.

RIGHTEOUSNESS IN ACTION

Throughout the New Testament, there is always this insistence on the practical. Colossians ii. 6—" As ye have received CHRIST JESUS the Lord, so walk ye in Him "—we are to walk what we talk. Romans i. 7—" Called to be saints "—we are to be what we are. John xiii. 17—" If ye know these things, happy are ye if ye do them "—we are to do what we know. Matthew vii. 21—" not everyone that saith . . . but he that doeth " ; Matthew xxiii. 3—" they say, and do not "—we are to practice what we say. So we are not surprised to find the same emphasis in this 10th verse—" whosoever doeth not righteousness is not of GOD ". We are not only to *be* righteous, but to *do* righteousness.

Herein lies one of the great differentiations between " the children of GOD " and " the children of the devil ". Whatever a man professes, if you find that he neglects the doing of righteous acts, the walking in righteous ways, you have every right to assume that he is not a righteous man, not a Christian. He may be one, of a very poor and unsatisfactory sort, but there is no evidence of it ; and as " by their fruits ye shall know them " it is more than likely that they are not " trees of righteousness, the planting of the LORD ", Isaiah lxi. 3, at all, however beautiful their " leaves ", Matthew xxi. 19, of profession may be. " Manifest ", therefore, the reality of your testimony by the fruits of good living, " that He may be glorified ", as the Isaiah verse finishes. But there is here something very striking.

There is not only one class of people—as is asserted so often, in a certain circle, who say that we are all GOD's children. Here, in the inspired record, is the plain division and distinction drawn, through the ranks of human society, " children of GOD " and " children of the devil ". Paul had inferred the same thing years before, when he described the condition of those who were then Christians as having " sometime " been " children of disobedience ", and " children of wrath " (Ephesians ii. 2–3), before they became, by New Birth, children of GOD. Indeed, did not the Saviour Himself accuse His adversaries, " Ye are of your father, the devil ", John viii. 44 ? Note next that *there are not three classes of people*— as if, not belonging to either of the two divisions, there were some middle-of-the-road position, a kind of neutrality. Hebrews ii. 3, " How shall we escape if we neglect so great salvation ", should suffice to guard anyone from resting upon such a supposition. Those who *reject* shall not escape ; but to *neglect* is, in effect, the same thing—for in either case we have not got it. Westcott, than whom there is no greater commentator on this Epistle, has drawn attention to the fact that " St. John divides the world sharply into two classes. Looking at the spiritual characteristics of life he admits no intermediate class. For him there is only light and darkness, and no twilight. He sees only life and death." May we venture to add—only white or black ; no grey. Thank GOD, *there is a choice of class for all people.* In the field of life there are only wheat and tares, and the latter can never have change of heart and nature to grow into the former category. They must remain unalterably, inexorably, the same " until the harvest ", Matthew xiii. 30, of Barn, or Burning.

But what is impossible in the natural world is gloriously possible in the spiritual realm. Though born, as we all are, into the bad family, as Psalm li. 5 will not allow us to forget, we can be born again into the good Family and Fellowship of GOD. Only remember that anyone whose life is not set to do righteously is manifestly not of GOD.

LOVE IN ACTION

Love is more than an emotional thing—it is intensely motional, especially in that highest form of it of which Paul speaks in II Corinthians v. 14, " The love of CHRIST constraineth us " : such love urged him on to " do exploits ", Daniel xi. 32. Love must do something, must give, in costly measure. Was it not so with GOD Himself—" For GOD so loved . . . that He gave . . .", John iii. 16.

Love is a fundamental thing—" This is the message that ye

heard from the beginning " (11). Though so little grasped, it is in reality one of the first, basic lessons in the Primary Division of the School of CHRIST—like " A.B.C. ", or " Twice Two are Four ", in the ordinary school. From the very beginning of their discipleship, as one of the First Steps in Christian Life Grammar, they had been instructed " that we should love one another ". And that is the case with all who have ever entered His school at all—as Paul puts it in another connection. " If so be that ye have heard Him, and have been taught by Him ", Ephesians iv. 21. And is not that apostle saying the same thing when he writes, " Learn first to show piety at home ", I Timothy v. 4. " Piety " there is love in action, and it is to be one of the priorities of Christian behaviour—it is a fundamental. It is an old Lesson, which has been taught to scholars ever since the School was opened, and newly taught to every new boy, or new girl, ever since, ii. 7–8.

Love is a natural thing—as between brethren. That is an unnatural family in which the boys are constantly quarrelling, and even thoroughly disliking each other. So it was with Cain (12). He couldn't stand young Abel, the " good boy " of the household, while he was the " bad lad ". Really nasty people often hate really nice people—" because " their very excellences show up their own depravities. How Judas hated JESUS. This is why real, all-out Christians should " marvel not if the world hate you " (13). What we should be surprised at is to find Christian " brethren " acting in an unbrotherly way towards their fellows. Alas, alas, alas—a not uncommon thing in many congregations. " Sirs, ye are brethren ; why do ye wrong one to another ? " Acts vii. 26. Yes, Moses knew right, and spake true. It is, indeed, a natural thing that we Christians should show a mutual affection—not only by avoiding wrongdoing to all, but by seeking well-being of each.

Love is a practical thing—as this whole passage so clearly and so constantly underlines. The fact of this frequent stress shows what importance GOD, the HOLY SPIRIT, attaches to it. Though there is high and deep sentiment in love, it is not merely sentimental. The true assessment of its quality lies, not in what we say, but in what it leads us to do. Take this, for example—" If ye love Me, ye will keep My commandments ", John xiv. 15, R.V. If we really love anyone their wish is a command ; and we may say of them as this Epistle

says of the LORD, " His commandments are not grievous ",
I John v. 3.   A stranger met a small girl carrying her little
brother and said, " What a burden you've got there ".   To
which the child replied, " This isn't a burden, it's my brother ".
A load gladly borne, almost bereft of weight, because she
loved.   That is love's way.

Love is an evidential thing—the possession of it will indicate
for us something of very great importance, which it will cause
us to " know ".   Do you want to know whether you have
passed from death to life ?   Here is one mark by which you
may test yourself—" because we love the brethren " (v. 14).
This is not the cause of the translation, but a sign of it.   It
is not without significance that, before " death " and " life ",
the Greek of the phrase has a definite article in each case.
It is not ordinary death that is meant, but " the " death—
that which entered into human experience at Eden, and whose
dread entail has since become part of the very being of us
all, the make-up of our human personality.   " As by one man
sin entered into the world, and death by sin ; and so death
passed upon all men . . .", Romans v. 12.   It is that particular
kind of death which characterises, and stigmatises, every
unregenerate soul as being " dead in trespasses and sins ",
Ephesians ii. 1.   It is that state which, unrepented of, is the
prelude of eventual and eternal " second death ", Revelation
xx. 14.   Ay, but there is a blessed alternative—" the " life :
that special species so often described as " eternal life ", and
of which the Master was thinking when He said, " I am come
that they might have life, and that they might have it more
abundantly ", John x. 10.   Well now, have we been trans-
ferred from that death to that life ?   Here's a simple test by
which we may " know "—Love !   Incidentally, it is also the
evidence, the test, by which the world may " know " where
we stand—" By this shall all men know that ye are My
disciples, if ye have love one to another ", John xiii. 35.   So
we observe that, on top of everything else, this practical love
has great evidential value—to our own hearts, and to the
estimate of others.

SACRIFICE IN ACTION

Here, indeed, is love at its highest—to the limit of an active
self-sacrifice.   Two persons, as it were, are involved in the

narrative—" He ", and " We " (16). *His Example is Para-mount*—" Hereby perceive we the love of GOD, because He laid down His life for us." This is not the expiatory aspect of His death—in that we could never have a part—but the exemplary aspect of it. We might, not unprofitably, stay a moment at that word " for " in this verse. In connection with the relationship to us of His atoning death, two quite different Greek prepositions are translated " for ", and they have entirely distinct meanings. To illustrate, look at these two seemingly contrary verses—(1) " Who gave Himself a ransom for *all* ", I Timothy ii. 6. (2) " To give His life a ransom for *many* ", Matthew xx. 28. Well, which is it : all, or many ? As so often in Scripture with apparently contra-dictory statements, the answer is, Both ; and the solution lies in the different prepositions used in the original. The first " for " means : on behalf of—indeed, He died on behalf of all. The second " for " means : instead of—in very truth, He died instead of many, not of all. One of the teachings that the devil hates is this doctrine of what is known as the Sub-stitutionary Atonement. Alas, there are many preachers to-day who reject it. Whereas it seems to me that the Bible is shot through with it. But—do you see the distinction between the two " fors " ? Let us take a simple illustration. A half-dozen people, non-swimmers, are fallen into the sea, and are in peril of drowning in the dangerously rough waves. A man, at grave risk to himself, gets a boat out. By pro-digious efforts, he manages to haul two into the boat and take them to safety. On going back, exhausted, for others, he is himself engulfed in the waters, giving his life on *behalf* of all six, but *instead* of the two—the four lost their own lives, his was not given instead of theirs, though on behalf of them. Is that clear ? In our verse, the preposition is " on behalf of " us.

In the second half of the verse we have a corollary. *His Expectation is Clear*—" we ought to lay down our lives for the brethren ". Not, of course, in dying for them, as He did on the Cross, but in living for them, as He did in His life. There is a further interesting grammatical point arising here. He " laid down " is in the Greek tense which signifies that it was done once for all, at a specific moment, as is so abundantly clear throughout the Epistle to the Hebrews—as, for instance, in x. 12, " after He had offered one sacrifice for sins for ever, sat down on the right hand of God ", as token that the sacrifice was complete : in His own word, " Finished ", John xix. 30. All that talk in certain circles about " the re-offering of the sacrifice " at Communion time is entirely unwarranted, in the face of Holy Scripture. When we turn, in our verse, to we " lay down ", we find a different Greek tense, the present, which signifies, not a " once for all " transaction, but a continual process. Our minds go at once to the challenging words of Romans xii. 1—" I beseech you therefore, brethren, by the mercies of GOD, that ye present your bodies a living sacrifice . . ." . His mercies exhibited in His laying down His in death for us is to be the motive, the incentive, to our laying down our bodies in life for others. The figure is drawn, of course, from the Old Testament sacrifice of the Burnt Offering, the only one of the Five in which everything was offered, nothing being kept back. Our offering of ourselves is to be exactly like that, with the one exception, that, whereas they became dead sacrifices, ours is to be a living sacrifice—a complete laying out of our lives in the service of GOD, and of " the brethren ". And that brings us on naturally to the last thought in this passage—

KINDNESS IN ACTION

Here is love in homespun—the doing of the little things, the giving of the cup of cold water in His Name, Matthew x. 42, the small touches that can mean so much. Indeed, it is no exaggeration to say that kindness can be a great evangelising agency—you say you can't work, you can't speak ; well, can you be kind ? A smile, a word, a touch—such things can be as seeds, which, in many an instance, have produced a golden harvest in a truly converted soul : the first impression having been made, the first inclination aroused, by some simple act of kindness. Wherefore, " be ye kind one to another ", Ephesians iv. 32. Perhaps that would be a good way of beginning to win your next-door neighbour to GOD ?

First, then, we have *The Need*—" his brother have need " (17). It is one of the many lovely characteristics of the Master that need was so powerful a magnet, drawing Him alongside—water couldn't keep Him away, Matthew xiv. 25 ; bolted doors couldn't bar His coming, John xx. 19 ; in an earlier day, fire couldn't prevent His approach to them, Daniel iii. 25.

And " this same JESUS ", living and loving as of yore, is
drawn by our need. But the point of this passage is, are we
so drawn, for there is plenty of need around. " We couldn't
care less " is, unfortunately, the attitude of many from their
own selfish ease and comfort. Needs of body, needs of heart,
needs of mind, needs of circumstance, needs of soul—well,
what about it ?

We have here, next, *The Heed*—" whoso . . . seeth ". There
is a certain force about that verb as if to suggest something
more than a mere, casual, passing glance, registering nothing
particular in the observer's mind—like the " certain priest "
in the Immortal Parable, Luke x. 31. The victim is shown
as " stripped . . . wounded . . . and half-dead " : need indeed.
But this was nothing to the reverend gentleman, he never
gave it a second thought. I used to think that, going to his
duties in the Temple at Jerusalem, he was afraid that contact
with this seemingly dead body would ceremonially disqualify
him from his priestly duties, which would have been the case
—until I noted that he was not going up, but that he " came
down ", his term of office was done, Luke i. 8. He just didn't
care : that was all, he took no heed of desperate need. It
was different, possibly worse, with the Levite following. He
did take the trouble to cross the road, and have a good look
at him, but he did nothing either—" poor fellow ", he would
say, sentimentally, as he " passed by ". Well, do you know
anything about that kind of attitude to need ?

So our verse carries on to suggest *The Deed*—not commend-
ing the " shutteth up his compassion ", but rather hinting
at the reverse, and, as it were, applauding the wholehearted
deed of the Good Samaritan, who " when he saw him, had
compassion on him ". Unknown, as he was ; unattractive,
as he must have looked ; unremunerative, as he was perforce
bound to be ; unfriendly, as " the Jews have no dealings with
the Samaritans ", John iv. 9—yes, he had plenty of reasons
for passing by on the other side. So had our Saviour, the
Ideal of the Good Samaritan, Who " when we were yet without
strength . . . while we were yet sinners . . . when we were
enemies,", died to save us, Romans v. 6, 8, 10. It was not
as if the man in our Epistle was in no position to help, for he
" hath this world's good "—he could, but would not.

A certain " sermon-taster " had heard that a celebrated
preacher was to be in a local church ; but, not knowing which

one, he spent most of the service time going unsuccessfully from place to place. At last he reached his target, with the great name placarded outside. As he approached, they were singing, and anxiously he wondered whether it was the hymn before or after. Putting his head inside the door, he asked someone, " Is the sermon done ? " To which he obtained the suggestive reply, " No, it's got to be done ". We hope it is not irreverent to hazard the view that that story would greatly have appealed to the New Testament writer who said, " Be ye doers of the word, and not hearers only ", James i. 22.

After all, the concluding verse of this section (18) sums up the whole matter of the practicality of the Fellowship when it says, " My little children, let us not love in word, neither in tongue ; but in deed and in truth ". So be it !

IX

THE PROOFS OF THE FELLOWSHIP

19 And hereby we know that we are of the truth, and shall assure our hearts before him.

20 For if our heart condemn us, God is greater than our heart, and knoweth all things.

21 Beloved, if our heart condemn us not, *then* have we confidence toward God.

22 And whatsoever we ask, we receive of him, because we keep his commandments, and do those things that are pleasing in his sight.

23 And this is his commandment, That we should believe on the name of his Son Jesus Christ, and love one another, as he gave us commandment.

24 And he that keepeth his commandments dwelleth in him, and he in him. And hereby we know that he abideth in us, by the Spirit which he hath given us.

1 Beloved, believe not every spirit, but try the spirits whether they are of God : because many false prophets are gone out into the world.

2 Hereby know ye the Spirit of God : Every spirit that confesseth that Jesus Christ is come in the flesh is of God :

3 And every spirit that confesseth not that Jesus Christ is come in the flesh is not of God : and this is that *spirit* of antichrist, whereof ye have heard that it should come ; and even now already is it in the world.

4 Ye are of God, little children, and have overcome them : because greater is he that is in you, than he that is in the world.

5 They are of the world : therefore speak they of the world, and the world heareth them.

6 We are of God : he that knoweth God heareth us ; he that is not of God heareth not us. Hereby know we the spirit of truth, and the spirit of error.

IN iv. 1 we have the word " try ". It is a technical word, used of the testing, or assaying, of metals to see if they ring true, or are up to standard. Our passage provides us with certain formulæ whereby we may test the realities of things, certain proofs whereby the members of the Fellowship may discern and differentiate between the genuine and the false. Note that phrase, " Hereby ye know "—it comes here four times ; and on each occasion it introduces what is the acid test of truth.

THE TEST OF THE TRUE SOUL

" Hereby we know that we are of the truth " (19)—that we are truly His. Let us not start testing others; we don't know their hearts, only GOD does. But let us be thorough, and fearless in testing ourselves. How then are we to know this ? The phrase apparently connects up with what has just been said, in the previous verses, and refers to the possession, and practice, of a loving Christian spirit.

" *If our heart condemn us* "—if we are conscious of some partial, or momentary, failure in the Christian temper, what then ? Does that mean that we no longer love Him, and have forfeited our right to His Name ? The fault must, of course, be confessed, and repented of, and thus be forgiven ; and then we may leave the matter with GOD, Who is " greater than our heart, and knoweth all things "—Who, because He understands, undertakes. Do you recall that poignant utterance of Peter, in that after-breakfast interview with his Risen Lord, Whom he had so basely denied—three times then he quailed, three times now is he questioned as to the real nature of his love. At last he breaks out with the heart-broken words, " LORD, Thou knowest all things, Thou knowest that I love Thee ", John xxi. 17. Yes, in spite of it all, the Master knew—and still knows, though we fall, if our love is true : the not falling is the test whereby *we* may know.

" *If our heart condemn us not* "—it is evident that the word " heart " is meant to be taken almost as the equivalent of conscience ; and it is presumed that that conscience is in a good condition. Let us beware of supposing that conscience is the voice of GOD, as some people assume. It is certainly His gift to man, like all other elements of his make-up—but, like the fingers that can steal, or the feet that can stray, this function also can go sadly awry. Under the stress of conscience many evils and cruelties have been perpetrated, as in times of religious persecution, as in the case of Saul of Tarsus—" I verily thought with myself that I *ought* to do many things contrary to the Name of JESUS ", Acts xxvi. 9. It is good to find this same man, now in his regenerate days, declaring, " herein I do exercise myself, to have always a conscience void of offence toward GOD, and toward men ", Acts xxiv. 16. Our conscience, then, can be seared, by doing despite to it ; it can be silenced, like your alarm clock, if you persistently disregard its morning summons ; it can act ignorantly, if it be not educated by the teaching of the Word of GOD—" ye do err, not knowing the Holy Scripture ", Matthew xxii. 29, says the Master to His foes. John Milton has a vivid metaphor for conscience in his *Paradise Lost*, he calls it " the umpire of the soul ". All we cricketers know how mistaken an umpire can be, through ignorance of the Laws of the Game, for instance. Let us, then, be careful to train our conscience by continually exercising ourselves in Bible truth. A sensitive conscience is one of the best blessings that a man can have—and the members of the Fellowship in our verse 21 are presumed to possess that quality, and finding themselves held innocent by that exact inquisitor, they are " assured " (19) of the " true " verdict of the Great Judge.

THE TEST OF THE TRUE INTERCESSOR

Nothing of all the activity of the members of the Fellowship is of greater importance than this ministry of intercession ; and because, for the due exercise of it, we must depend so largely upon GOD, we read " Hereby we know that He abideth in us " (24). Here is the guarantee to us of the truth of that sublime benefit : " The SPIRIT which He hath given us "— the Divine Donation vouchsafed to every Christian, for " if any man have not the SPIRIT of CHRIST, he is none of His ", Romans viii. 9. And the special relation of the Divine Third Person to our life of true intercession is seen in this same chapter of the Roman Epistle (viii. 26), " Likewise the SPIRIT also helpeth our infirmities : for we know not what we should pray for as we ought ; but the SPIRIT Himself maketh intercession [in] us ". Think, then, of some of the striking things that He has here caused John to write for the guidance and encouragement of GOD's true intercessors.

The Statement—" whatsoever we ask, we receive of Him " (22). That is a sweeping assertion ; but, nevertheless, let us be quite confident that the " receiving " is all right if the " asking " is all right. The " whatsoever " is here stated ; the " howsoever " is implied—a right asking is concerned, not only with the matter, but also with the manner. Let us mark at this point that there is a stage of spiritual development in the experience of the true, SPIRIT-guided intercessor in which he may be sure that his prayers shall be answered.

The Condition—" because we keep His commandments, and do those things that are pleasing in His sight ". It is a truism that GOD always keeps His promises : we may put our finger —indeed our whole being—on it, and rest upon His fidelity to His pledged word. But, wait ! Before you are in a position to do that, you must remember that almost, if not quite, without exception, the promises of GOD are not unconditional, and their fulfilment is dependent upon such conditions. Promise and proviso go in pairs—if we keep the second, He will keep the first. There are several conditions attaching to GOD's gracious undertaking to answer our petitions. What is, perhaps, the chiefest of them is the one that is enunciated here—the all-important " because " ! It all depends upon our attitude towards Him : an obedient conduct, and a pleasing behaviour. A prayer that is acceptable and answered is dependent, not on diligence, nor on eloquence ; but, quite simply, on obedience.

The Explanation—is to be noted of what John implies in his use of that word " commandments ". Lest we should suppose that if we do not keep the Ten Commandments, our prayers will be neither heard nor heeded, he hastens to explain what he means. " This is His commandment " (23)—notice that, though he is citing two, he conceives them as one, as if they hung together. " Believe " Him ; " love " others—the first the source of the second ; the second the sign of the first. Here is the twofold secret of His manifold answers.

The Atmosphere—in which effectual prayer flourishes is now stated, " dwelleth in Him, and He in him " (24). How true it is that we never really know people until we live with them. Residing there, we get to know their mind about things, and instinctively realise what we might ask for. Suppose you were " fond of a glass ", and discovered that the people you had gone to live with were staunch teetotallers —you would know, wouldn't you, what you must not ask for ? I hope this is not a ribald illustration of the point we are at in our present study. GOD has allowed our deeply privileged intimacy with Him to be described under the figure of two " dwelling " together—" he in Him, and He in him ". It is in this wondrous nearness that " we have the mind of CHRIST ", I Corinthians ii. 16, and become aware, as if by instinct, of the things He would have us ask for, and so

" whatsoever we ask, we receive of Him ". Reader and writer : shall we pray for one another that we may attain to such a fruitful understanding of the Divine mind ?

THE TEST OF THE TRUE SPIRIT

There are many spirits abroad in the world to-day angling for our adherence and allegiance ; and there is a type of Christian, ill-instructed in the Scriptures (which, incidentally, the wrong spirits misquote *ad lib.*), who are only too readily gullible to every front-door exponent of false teaching—only too liable to " believe every spirit " (iv. 1). Apparently, it was very much the same in John's day ; and, under Divine guidance, he offers the members of the Fellowship (now, as well as then) an acid test whereby the real nature, whether true or false, can be determined. " Hereby know ye the SPIRIT of GOD " (2). Try this next time they come to your doorstep !

What, then, is the Test ? " Every spirit that confesseth that JESUS CHRIST is come in the flesh is of GOD, and every spirit that confesseth not . . . is not of GOD, and this is that spirit of antichrist " (2–3) For many years this passage troubled me, because I could not see why such tremendous issues should hang upon so simple a thing as the acknowledgment that JESUS CHRIST was an historical personage. Of course He was : even these false spirits will agree to that. Secular historians, quite independently of the Bible—Josephus, Pliny, for instance—record the fact. At last I thought I saw my way out—if only it were justifiable to translate the Greek differently from the Authorised Version, by placing the little " is " in another position. Was I right ? Some time back, I came into touch with a profound Greek scholar, and to my great glee, he said that my rendering of the original was perfectly allowable.

Before giving you my conviction, let me remind you that " JESUS " is the Name of the Master's Humanity, and that " CHRIST " is the title of His Deity, the Divine anointed One come to be the promised and predicted Messiah, Saviour, and King. Do you see now what I am driving at ? Yes ; this is the suggested translation," Every spirit that confesseth that JESUS is CHRIST come in the flesh . . .". An acknowledgment, you see, of His Deity. Chapter v. 1 of the Epistle supports

my interpretation, doesn't it ?   And the first and fundamental test of every spirit claiming to be of GOD is, " What
think ye of CHRIST ? " Matthew xxii. 42.   If you are satisfied
that they believe that He was more than a wonderful, remarkable Man, more than a unique Man, the Best ever, that,
indeed, they confess to a belief in His true, real, complete
Deity—then you can proceed to a further examination.   If
they do not hold this belief, this passage justifies you—even
instructs you—to close the interview.   Waste no further
time !

What, then, is the believer's attitude ?   One of hostility, and
of victory.   Not through their own cleverness is this to be ;
but by a threefold secret (4).   (1) *A relationship*—" ye are of
GOD ".   You are His, and, therefore, on His side.   Even if,
in your own circumstances, you stand alone, the only real
Christian, facing opposition, engendered by these ungodly
spirits, you may remember that even " one with GOD is a
majority ".   (2) *A result*—" ye have overcome them ".   Of
course, because His is the winning side ; and if you keep
faith with Him, He will keep faith with you.   What joy !
What thrill—to be on the Victory Side.   The sign whereof
is not a " V ", but an empty Cross !   (3) *A reason*—the Divine
indwelling.   " Greater is He that is in you, than he that is
in the world ".   Because the Victor abides in us, we can be
victors over all the powers of darkness, and his emissaries
" in the world ".

THE TEST OF THE TRUE TEACHER

Here the apostle passes over from the spirits of antichrist
to the persons in whom they are manifested ; or, if you like,
from the teaching to the teacher.   " Hereby know we the
spirit of truth, and the spirit of error " (6).   The two orders
of teachers may be recognised each for what they are in themselves, and by the spirit with which they are imbued.   Examine
these teachers, then.

The Test is not Popularity.   The false teachers may attract
to themselves great congregations, they may enjoy a good
press, they may get satisfying preferment, and may be reckoned as highly successful—so runs the record, " the world
heareth them ".   Of course, popularity is not necessarily a
sign of falsity.   Many a true teacher has been a popular

preacher ; and some of the biggest congregations to-day are ministered by faithful pastors. We are only saying that a big following is not, either way, the proof of a sound teacher. The worldling preacher (5) is " of the world "—his standards are those of the world ; his viewpoint is surprisingly worldly ; his power is largely vested in worldly attributes ; his appeal is pretty much to the world. " Therefore ", they are popular there. The members of the Fellowship will not be misled ; they will be on their guard against measuring true success by so erroneous a test.

The Test is, after all, Spirituality. These teachers are not worldlings, but godly. GOD is their aim, their message, their power, their joy. The world turns from them with scorn, if not with amusement, and rates them Bible-punchers. Bible-preachers they certainly are, who rest on the Scriptures, not " wrest " them, II Peter iii. 16, as the false teachers do ; for, as Shakespeare knowingly reminds us, " the devil can quote Scriptures to his purpose "—though he generally gets it wrong, as in Matthew iv. 6 compared with Psalm xci. 11. " He that knoweth GOD heareth us " (6), claims the apostle—the congregation recognise the accent, and at once perceive the truth. This is beyond us, says the worldling, what is the man driving at ? This is of GOD, says the heavenly citizen, we would know that speech anywhere. If you, my reader, are a preacher, or teacher, would this not be a proper yearning of your heart—

> " O that it might be said of me,
> Surely thy speech bewrayeth thee,
> Thou hast been with JESUS of Galilee,
> With JESUS of Galilee."

X

THE POSITION OF THE FELLOWSHIP

I JOHN iv. 7-21

7 Beloved, let us love one another : for love is of God ; and every one that loveth is born of God, and knoweth God.

8 He that loveth not knoweth not God ; for God is love.

9 In this was manifested the love of God toward us, because that God sent his only begotten Son into the world, that we might live through him.

10 Herein is love, not that we loved God, but that he loved us, and sent his Son *to be* the propitiation for our sins.

11 Beloved, if God so loved us, we ought also to love one another.

12 No man hath seen God at any time. If we love one another, God dwelleth in us, and his love is perfected in us.

13 Hereby know we that we dwell in him, and he in us, because he hath given us of his Spirit.

14 And we have seen and do testify that the Father sent the Son *to be* the Saviour of the world.

15 Whosoever shall confess that Jesus is the Son of God, God dwelleth in him, and he in God.

16 And we have known and believed the love that God hath to us. God is love ; and he that dwelleth in love dwelleth in God, and God in him.

17 Herein is our love made perfect, that we may have boldness in the day of judgment : because as he is, so are we in this world.

18 There is no fear in love ; but perfect love casteth out fear : because fear hath torment. He that feareth is not made perfect in love.

19 We love him, because he first loved us.

20 If a man say, I love God, and hateth his brother, he is a liar : for he that loveth not his brother whom he hath seen, how can he love God whom he hath not seen ?

21 And this commandment have we from him, That he who loveth God love his brother also.

WHAT a very great influence, both in the formation of our character, and in the experience of life, our dwelling-place has upon us—our neighbourhood, and our own home. There has often been good argument as to which is the stronger— heredity, or environment. I fancy that, nowadays, the pundits are inclined to give it to the latter, so tremendous is the pull and power of the conditions of our habitation. The same rule holds in the spiritual sphere ; and this passage deals with the Christian's position here below.　" We seek a city " yonder, Hebrews xiii. 14 ; but the Epistle is concerned with the earthly dwelling of the soul.　Our portion speaks of the member of the Fellowship having three places that he lives " in ".　One is reminded of the spacious days when the well-to-do had several houses for their enjoyment.　In his delightful and revealing essays on " Great Contemporaries ", Sir Winston Churchill has a study of the late Earl of Rosebery, in the course of which he says, " I was often his guest in all his houses, at Mentmore, in Berkeley Square, at the Durdans hard by Epsom Downs, on the Firth of Forth at Dalmeny, at his shooting-lodge, Rosebery "—well, well !　Still, with all these, his life—if I may be pardoned an impertinent allusion to his family name—was along no Primrose path.　So we turn to our consideration of the three dwelling-places of the believers, and mark what are their consequent responsibilities, difficulties, and blessings in such a position as theirs.

THEIR SOCIAL POSITION

　　" In this world " (17).　*The world is an alien country*—so that, in the Lord's Prayer, he says, " They are not of the world ", John xvii. 16.　Yet He has said, " I pray not that Thou shouldest take them out of the world, but that Thou shouldest keep them from the evil ".　In moments of depression, we might wish that immediately upon our New Birth we were granted the administration of our Supernaturalisation Papers and were there and then transported to our now native country up yonder.　But what adventure for GOD we should then miss ; what possible honours in the fight for Him we should fail to achieve !　So we are left here, and may exercise in our residence so great an influence for good, and for GOD. One day, in an electric moment of time, all the believers *will be* taken out of the world—those who have died, and those who are alive at the moment, all suddenly transformed and transported, to be " for ever with the LORD ", I Thessalonians iv. 16–17.　A queer situation will then arise on the earth the moment after it has happened, that differentiating as between believers and unbelievers, living and working closely together, " one shall be taken, and the other left ", Luke xvii. 34–6.

　　Meanwhile, it is to be remembered that *the world is a field of infection*—" that Thou shouldest keep them from the evil ". For our safeguard we must continually be on guard, for the virulent germs of evil thinking, evil speaking, and evil doing are for ever poisoning the spiritual atmosphere, and we shall succumb, unless we allow ourselves to be " kept " immune by the deodorising effects of the HOLY SPIRIT, and by the disinfecting power of the Holy Scriptures. We are told that the best defence is attack ; and so it is made clear to us that we are to exercise a positive influence wherever we are—even as the Saviour taught, as we have said earlier, that we are to be as " salt " to prevent corruption, as " light " to bring cheer and guidance, and as a hill-top " city " to give clear testimony to Him. Here we are, then, living in this difficult environment—living to serve Him, and to help others. There is still another New Testament figure of the Christian in an alien country which is, again, full of significance—" we are ambassadors for CHRIST ", II Corinthians v. 20. Earthly monarchs have their ambassadors in other lands, to represent them at the foreign court—standing for the dignities and rights of their Sovereign, keeping their Government in touch with anything affecting the interests of their Country, speaking in the Name of their Ruler, and with all his Power behind them. All that lies within the ambassadorial figure that Paul here employs, to indicate still another aspect of our responsibility as representing our Sovereign Lord to those among whom we live " in this world ".

That leads on to the further thought that *the world is a great audience*—before which we are engaged to enact a special performance. In I Corinthians iv. 9 we read that " we are made a spectacle unto the world ", where the original word for " spectacle " is the word from which our " theater "comes. We are as a theater with the world looking on. Our representation of Him is a History, if it is a true likeness ; a Comedy, if we burlesque the great part we are meant to play ; a Tragedy, if we sadly misrepresent Him to the audience. Turn now to our passage and note its expression of this idea. We read that " as He is, so are we in this world " (17). Not, you observe, as He *was*, but *is* even now in His Divine omnipresence, though to the world-audience unseen—the rôle is, that they shall see JESUS in us. How searching are the simple words of the chorus, " Can others see JESUS in me ? " Well—can they ? Are we, by His grace, acting the part well. I believe that actors on the ordinary stage are successful in so far as they faithfully study their part. All right then—" consider Him ", Hebrews xii. 3, and act accordingly. There is another verse in our passage, along the same lines—" No man hath seen GOD at any time. If we love one another, GOD dwelleth in us . . ." (12). The first sentence seems to hang in mid-air, having no connection with what comes before, or after. But upon reflection it seems to me that the argument is after the same pattern as in verse 17—GOD is not seen in Himself ; but, if we display the spirit of love, people can see Him in us. Does not this thought place upon us a tremendous responsibility to see that, as we considered in our sixth study, the portrait is clearly recognised, and, as here, that the performance is true to life.

Here, then, we learn something of the calls and claims resting upon the members of the Fellowship, on account of their social position, as residing " in this world ". Let us go on to look at their second dwelling—so utterly and beautifully contrasted as it is.

THEIR SPIRITUAL POSITION

" In love " (16). The whole passage is full of references to, descriptions of, and blessings in, the Love House—an exquisitely delightful residence. Double-fronted—love to GOD, love to others. Long lease—even for eternity. Sunny aspect —constantly lit by the Sun of Righteousness. Every modern convenience—for " love never faileth ". Safe from disturbance—for " perfect love casteth out fear ". Note that the phrase employed is " dwelleth in love ", not " lodgeth ", as if for a while—there is all the difference between visiting the seaside for a holiday, and living there permanently. It is this latter condition that is envisaged here. The house itself is a permanency—" now abideth . . . love ", I Corinthians xiii. 13 —and we are never to move elsewhere.

We are said to be Born there—" born of GOD " (7). Not by natural birth, but by new birth. In the beautiful atmosphere where love reigns—that is, in effect, where GOD reigns, for " GOD is love "—there is no room for a spirit of hate, a spirit of fear, a spirit of greed, a spirit of jealousy, a spirit of self. It is a sign of a newly born body that it breathes life ; likewise is it a mark of a new born soul that it breathes love—

for we cannot really know GOD without catching from Him
some of His wonderful spirit of love (8).

We are said to Grow there—" herein is our love made perfect " (17).   Love is not a merely static thing, but is for ever
growing deeper as the days go by—from the cupboard love
of the cat, to the childish love of the infant, the callow love
of the youth, the awakening love of the sweetheart, the deepening love of a married couple, to the perfect love of a Darby
and Joan. So does it come about, in the higher sphere, that
the more we know GOD the more we love Him—and, incidentally, the more we love others. As the Christian should be
always on the go, so should he also be always on the grow—
" as newborn babes, desire the sincere [the unadultered] milk
of the Word, that ye may grow thereby ", I Peter ii. 2. We
are to grow in all kinds of Christian excellencies—for instance,
in grace, in knowledge, and in love. This love that the Epistle
is so full of is a supernatural quality—" shed abroad in our
hearts [not by our effort] by the HOLY GHOST who is given
unto us ", Romans v. 5. The New Testament word for love
is not found in heathen writers ; and their word for it is not
found in the New Testament—though it is given an exalted
place in London's Piccadilly Circus ! Let us see to it that, as
members of the Fellowship we are growing in the Divine
virtue.

We are said to Live there—" dwelleth in love " (16). The
Love life follows a pattern, " manifested " in the blessed fact
that GOD sent His Son to be incarnate (9) and crucified (10)
for us. A strange word is used of the latter fact—" the propitiation " ; and we must give careful attention to it, in view
of certain strictures that occur in certain quarters. They begin
by quoting from this very Epistle, this very chapter, that
" GOD is love ". Very well, then, if that be the case, He will
surely forgive " our sins ", without any need to be propitiated
on account of them. Yet the Bible does describe the Cross,
not only as an example of love (how true !), but as a propitiation for sins. You see, there are two sides to the nature of
GOD, as revealed to us—" GOD is love ", iv. 8 ; but also,
" GOD is light ", i. 5, and the two must be held in balance.
The first word signifies, shall we say, His attitude towards
our highest good ; the second word embraces His attitude
against all evil—in consequence of this latter capacity, innate
in a Holy Deity, sin must be adequately dealt with. He

cannot, from the very nature of this side of His Being, deal
with it as if He were an easy-going, indulgent Father.   A
propitiation there must be—but note carefully the phrase
that He " sent . . . the propitiation ".   The same thought is
in Romans iii. 25-6, " Whom GOD sent forth to be a propitiation . . . that He might be [at the same time] just, and
the justifier ".   The Cross dealt with the sin, and delivered
the sinner who believed.   So that we come to this " righteous "
conclusion that, seeing there must be a propitiation, His love
provided what His holiness demanded !   " Herein is love "
(10)—indeed.

And now we have to remind ourselves that Life in Love
lays upon us the obligation to reproduce, in our measure, the
pattern of love that is set before us—not to do *what* He did,
which was uniquely His work, but to do *as* He did.   " Beloved,
if GOD so loved us, we ought also to love one another " (11).
" We love [the ' Him ' is to be omitted] because He first loved
us " (19).   It is no use our saying that the copy is too remote,
and the task too difficult, for, as we learned in an earlier
study, GOD never commands His children to do the impossible,
Exodus xviii. 23, and " this *commandment* have we from Him,
that he who loveth GOD love his brother also " (21).   This
rule of the household is His command ; the grace for the
doing of it is ours to command !   What further residence is
there for the members of the Fellowship ?

THEIR SUPERNATURAL POSITION

" In Him " (13)—a privileged position, beyond all human
comprehension, but not, thank GOD, beyond our apprehension.
You will recall that the phrase is one characteristic of Paul,
who constantly uses it—" in the LORD ", " in CHRIST ".   Led
of the SPIRIT, he confidently affirms that all that we Christians
have, or hope for, is because of our being " in Him ".   Such
a position brings us such a plethora of graces and blessings.
" We dwell in Him ", says John, " and He in us ", he adds ;
for there is, as we have seen, a reciprocal aspect about it—
if the poker is in the fire, the fire is soon in the poker ; if
the sponge is in the water, the water is in the sponge ; if the
body is in the air, the air is in the body—and, to infinitely
greater purpose, if we dwell in Him, He dwells in us.   It is
this second side of the coin that gives the value to the specie ;

and if only we recognise it, we shall be saved from so much spiritual collapse. Recall the low moral condition into which the Corinthian Christians had fallen, and note Paul's indication of its root cause—" What ? Know ye not that . . . the HOLY GHOST is in you " I Corinthians vi. 19. With the Holy One there they *ought* not, and *need* not, be unholy ; nor we !

What of the Old Home ? Of the unrepentant unbeliever, the threefold record runs : (1) " Born in sins ", John ix. 34— not true of our Lord, but true of all else. Do you remember the pathetic lines of poor Tom Hood, in his Past and Present—

" I remember, I remember, the house where I was born
The little window where the sun came peeping in at morn."

Spiritually, this was it : " born in sins ". If we are no longer there, let us thank GOD for the grace that moved us ; but, to continue, (2) " Lived in them ", Colossians iii. 7—all we believers lived there once, and what a life of disappointment it was ; what an unsafe and unsatisfactory house to be in. (3) " Die in your sins ", John viii. 24—there is the poignant Obituary Notice of the impenitent. That, then, is our original dwelling-place—in sin ; until we come to be—in Him.

What of the New Home ? How different from the old place. Here is love, and joy, and peace, and satisfaction, and service, and all blessing. Here we abide all the years of our earthly life—not only with Him, but in Him—until the great Removal Day when, in the mercy of GOD, we move into that other " house not made with hands, eternal in the heavens ", II Corinthians v. 1. Members of the Fellowship : how infinitely privileged we are in our Position, while Here—and when There.

XI

THE POWER OF THE FELLOWSHIP

I JOHN v. 1-5

1 Whosoever believeth that Jesus is the Christ is born of God : and every one that loveth him that begat loveth him also that is begotten of him.

2 By this we know that we love the children of God, when we love God, and keep his commandments.

3 For this is the love of God, that we keep his commandments : and his commandments are not grievous.

4 For whatsoever is born of God overcometh the world : and this is the victory that overcometh the world, *even* our faith.

5 Who is he that overcometh the world, but he that believeth that Jesus is the Son of God ?

THE true member of the Fellowship is potentially so strong because he possesses a secret whereby he can, if we may put it so, turn on the power as needed. Alas, many of us are so weak, such failures, because we fail to use the switch. This passage introduces to us the whole matter of this power. So, because we all long for power, we give earnest attention to what is said. What a sad difference there is between some Christians and others—the powerful and the powerless. If we belong to the latter class, maybe this study will be the means of transferring us to the former company. To our subject, then—

POWER—CRADLED IN LOVE

The apostle seems quite unable to get away from the subject of love—he conceives it to be of such vast and vital importance that all other excellencies rest on it, or spring from it, or are irradiated by it. Paul would most heartily approve such sentiments as the study of his unmatched pæan of love, in I Corinthians xiii., discloses. John can most appropriately be called the apostle of love. Yet how different a character he had been, even at the beginning of his apostolate. Think of Mark iii. 17, " James and John He surnamed, Boanerges,

Sons of Thunder ", such was their stormy disposition. There's not much affinity between love and a thunderstorm. Think of Mark ix. 38, " John answered, Master, we saw one casting out devils in Thy Name, and we forbad him, because he followeth not us ". A loveless attitude, rebuked by his Lord. Think of Luke ix. 54, " James and John said, Lord, wilt Thou that we command fire to come down from heaven, and consume them ? " There's a deep disparity between lightning and love. If ever there were an instance of the HOLY SPIRIT's completely transforming a man's whole nature, we find it in the case of this man John. " The fruit of the SPIRIT is love . . .", Galatians v. 22.

How amazing is the power of this gentle quality of love. You have seen illustrations of it in the field of nature. Yonder garden is wrapt in winter's grip, the icy cold has persisted long, and hardened all around. Snow now covers the ground. Yet, what is this that pokes up its little, delicate head at the foot of that tree ? What power does this tiny snowdrop possess, not only to endure, but even to triumph thus over all that winter can bring ? Such is love that can persist amid all the rigours and vigours of this oft-times cruel world. Look at that irregular stone in your pavement. What has lifted it like that ? Only a little seed dropped by a bird on to the earth before the stone was hammered into its place. That tiny, wee thing has lifted a weight immeasurably greater than its own. So can love lift the load that bows down many a heart, or raise the stone that hardens many a life. How often has the love of a mother's broken heart lingered on for her erring son when all other decent people have become ashamed of him and given him up. Love never gives up ; but " beareth all things . . . endureth all things ", I Corinthians xiii. 7.

We are not surprised, then, at the writer's reiteration. He brings before us again the two aspects of this heavenly characteristic. *First*, " every one that loveth him that begat " (1). It begins with love to GOD, all else springs from that. If He had not so loved the world as to send His only begotten Son to save us ; if He had not so loved us individually as to beget us in newness of life, and " unto a lively hope ", I Peter i. 3 ; if He had not " first loved us " (iv. 19), we could never have loved in this Divine way. But, first, our love is to be given to " Him that begat ", that, in His own Self, started it all. *Second*, " loveth him also that is begotten of Him "

We have heard the old saying, " Love me, love my dog ".
The idea here is similar : love GOD, love His child. Saint
Augustine held that this phrase referred to CHRIST, " the
only begotten of the Father ", John i. 14 ; but the late Bishop
Westcott felt that the whole context was against that interpretation, and that it must mean, not the Son but the sons.
" We know that we love the children of GOD, when we love
GOD " (2). And this is not so much a matter of choice as a
specific " commandment ", though this is understood to be,
and found to be, not a heavy burden, but a loving rule of the
Fellowship. He has said all this before, you say ? But can
it be said too often ? Our memories are so short, and our
natures so frail, that it would seem to be salutary to hear it
over and over again. Let him that is conscious of fulfilling
the twofold commandment complain of the repetition ; but
let us who are only too well aware of our shortcoming thank
GOD for the constant reminder. Our spiritual power, then,
is cradled in love. That which emanates from any other
source is likely to be hard, remorseless, and self-seeking.

POWER—INNATE FROM BIRTH

Physically, we watch with wonder the strength resident in
the tiny frame of the newly born babe as it battles with the
world into which it has come—a struggle which, as infant
mortality rates lessen, we know to be mostly successful.
Spiritually, how shall it be otherwise with those who are born
again—" for whatsoever is born of GOD overcometh the
world " (4). From the very moment of what we call our
conversion—but which, to be exact, we should call our regeneration—the power to be, to speak, to act, to serve, to
conquer, is there, if only we will use it. We are" born of the
SPIRIT ", John iii. 6, Who, from that time, is " in you ",
I Corinthians vi. 19—so that, from our earliest days of Christian life, strength sufficient to " overcome " is daily at our
disposal.

Turning aside for a moment, look at that distinction between
conversion and regeneration. We can be regenerated but
once ; we can be converted often—and so many, alas, need
to be. To convert is to turn back ; and a regenerated person
may stray from the narrow path. As often as he does so, he
will need to return into the straight. Some have asked if,

though chosen to be an apostle, Peter was not a converted man, and when was he converted, since the Master said, " and when thou art converted ", Luke xxii. 32. Oh yes, he was a regenerated man, a real Christian, but he would grievously stray. When he had turned back again, he was to give himself arduously to the strengthening of his fellow believers, lest they also fail and fall. If you are truly a backslider, you do not need to re-enter the Family (you are, once for all, regenerated), but to return to the Fellowship, whose sunlight you have forfeited (you are converted back from your wandering). We need, just now, to convert to our passage on spiritual strength—and to hear again that " ye shall receive power after that the HOLY GHOST is come upon you ", Acts i. 8, which happened to you at the instant of your regeneration.

POWER—AVAILABLE TO FAITH

" This is the victory that overcometh the world "—even our fighting ? No ; prepare for a surprise—" even our faith " (4). The interesting discovery, as we carefully study the New Testament, is that, while the beginning of our Christian life, so far as we are concerned, is in faith, the continuing of the same is likewise in faith, from start to finish. The principle of faith runs right through—that is our part in the matter. At the opening of this study, I spoke about a switch, for the utilising of the power that is there. This is the switch—Faith. I heard of an old lady who was scared of electricity, whom nothing and no one could induce to use a switch and turn on the power. As I have heard of some Christians who, in spite of spiritual failure, have never been persuaded to try the switch of faith—self-effort, at its best and fullest ; but never the Bible way " even our faith ". Let me try to expound this secret of power, as the Scriptures set it before us.

Power of Salvation—" By grace are ye saved through faith ", Ephesians ii. 8. Every real member of the Fellowship, every true Christian, will subscribe to that. He knows that salvation comes from GOD ; that He took the initiative ; that, at the tremendous cost of the Saviour's precious Blood, this mighty Rescue is possible for us ; that it is all of His " grace ", the wholly undeserved kindness of His loving heart. " By grace ", indeed—that, in the blessed entirety of it, is GOD's part in the great transaction. And our part ? Simply " through faith "—we have but to turn the switch ; and there is the light, the warmth, the power, that are summed up in the word and fact of salvation. Has my reader switched on ?

Power to Continue—" we walk by faith, not by sight ", II Corinthians v. 7. What we call our conversion is not merely a stopping place, but a starting place—" let us go on ", says Hebrews vi. 1. As we take our journey across the ocean of life there are things like storms, and rocks, and quicksands that would hinder, or even halt, our continuance. There are things that would help and hasten it, as chart, and compass, and helm, answering to the means of grace, such as the Bible, the Prayer, the Communion, the Fellowship, the Service, which explain why the Pentecostal converts " continued sted-fastly ", Acts ii. 42. But, after all, that ship cannot voyage on by what the passenger sees, but only by a force generated deep down, unseen—switched on no less than as is your little table lamp. A skipper, explaining what it was like in a storm, pictured the calm, still waters as the ship nosed her way out into the open sea. Then comes the tempest, he said, and every-thing seems against us—the now blackened sky, the mountain-ous waves, the pitiless rain, the howling wind. All speak with one frightening voice : they seem to say to me, and to my ship, " You shan't come ; you shan't come ; you shan't come ". But, he went on, I stand there on the bridge, tightly holding on to the rail, vibrating with the force of the engines down below. Thus while everything else threatens, " You shan't come ", the engines stoutly reply, " Yes, we will ; yes, we will ; yes, we will ". And, added the captain, so we do. Ay, fellow voyager, the secret is down there below in your innermost being—the means of grace may (and will) greatly help you on, but the master power is the HOLY GHOST power within, which you can only harness to your continuance by pressing the switch of faith.

Power to Understand—" by faith we understand ", Hebrews xi. 3. We have a phrase that " seeing is believing " ; but in the spiritual realm it is so often the opposite, that " believing is seeing ". There are things of the spirit that the worldling will never understand, because he starts by not believing them. This attitude of faith seems very odd to him. Of course it does, " for the natural man receiveth not the things of the SPIRIT of GOD, for they are foolishness unto him ; neither can he know them, because they are spiritually

discerned", I Corinthians ii. 14.   The new man takes the word
of GOD at its face value. He comes upon this thing. He says,
I don't understand it, but GOD says it, and I believe it ; and
presently he says, I see ! The switch of faith turns on the
light of truth.

Power of Sanctification—" them which are sanctified by
faith that is in Me ", Acts xxvi. 18.   The old dictum holds
for every Christian, " Be ye holy, for I am holy "—the same
in Old Testament requirement, Leviticus xi. 44, as in New,
I Peter i. 16.   And the detailed account of it is given as " love,
joy, peace, longsuffering, gentleness, goodness, faith, meek-
ness, control : that is real holiness, true sanctification.   Mark
that all this is obtained, not by our works, " the works of the
flesh " are very different, but as " the fruit of the SPIRIT ",
Galatians v. 22.   He who dwells within every true member of
the Fellowship produces, if we get out of His way, and trust
Him to do it, these lovely things.   The switch of faith turns
on the heat that ripens this glorious fruit.   This is the kernel
of what is known as the Keswick message : sanctification by
faith !

Power for Victory—" this is the victory that overcometh
the world, even our faith " (4).   The Lord had said to our
John, and to the rest, " Be of good cheer, I have overcome
the world ", John xvi. 33.   Shall we who are His, who indeed
are " in Him ", fight the battle all over again ?   Shall we not
then rather trust in what He has accomplished by His death
and rising again, and take from Him the conquest ?   In the
moment of our temptation, let us have done with struggling,
and instantly, by a deliberate act of faith, take the victory
already won, and in that moment made available to us.
Bishop Westcott, commenting on this passage, wrote words
that might have been uttered on the Keswick platform—
" The victory which the Christian is ever winning is the personal appropriation of a victory gained once for all ".   Says
Bishop Gore, " It is His victory appropriated by us ".   Victory
by faith : yes, that's it.   The switch of faith turns on the
power to overcome.

Power for Daily Life—" the life that I now live in the flesh,
I live by the faith of the Son of GOD ", Galatians ii. 20 : faith
on the Son of GOD is the meaning.   The life that some Christians now live is a life according to the flesh—the lower
nature ; or, according to the fashion—like a spiritual

chameleon ; or, according to the feelings—now up, now down ; but Paul lives according to faith on the Son of GOD. He has found that carried him through the big occasions, and the sudden emergencies. He would have us know that it is the power sufficient to meet the calls of the ordinary, unexciting, humdrum affairs of the day-to-day routine. I say ! What an electric switch is this faith. Have you learnt to use it ? So—

POWER—ISSUING IN VICTORY

This is the prospect held out to all Fellowship members—" who is he that overcometh the world, but he that believeth that JESUS is the Son of GOD ? " (5). That is, that trusts in faith to Him, Whom he knows to possess all the experience of perfect humanity, and all the unconquerable power of transcendant Deity. Such unfaltering reliance on Him will have a wonderful issue in the Christian's life—victory over sinful habits, victory over all temptations, victory over trying circumstances, victory over depressing feelings, victory over personal insufficiencies, victory over dominant self. Victory all along the line—by fighting for it ? No, no—" even our faith ". Verily, " if ye have faith . . . nothing shall be impossible unto you ", Matthew xvii. 20.

Then, where do I come in ? If you're wise, you don't ! The life of a small boy at school was made a misery by the bully. His elder brother was a senior prefect ; but, of course, the youngster couldn't " sneak ". One day the brother saw what was going on. The bully had his back to him, and didn't observe him advancing, but the victim did. So, dodging away, he ran behind his big brother, and looking through his arms akimbo, he said to his tormentor, " Now come on ! " The Boy, the Bully, and the Big Brother—there's the secret of victory there. Never was such a bully as Satan ; never such a Strong One as He Who " is not ashamed to call them brethren ", Hebrews ii. 11. Get behind Him, leave the antagonist to Him.

XII

THE POSSESSION OF THE FELLOWSHIP

6 This is he that came by water and blood, *even* Jesus Christ ; not by water only, but by water and blood. And it is the Spirit that beareth witness, because the Spirit is truth.

7 For there are three that bear record in heaven, the Father, the Word, and the Holy Ghost : and these three are one.

8 And there are three that bear witness in earth, the Spirit, and the water, and the blood : and these three agree in one.

9 If we receive the witness of men, the witness of God is greater : for this is the witness of God which he hath testified of his Son.

10 He that believeth on the Son of God hath the witness in himself : he that believeth not God hath made him a liar ; because he believeth not the record that God gave his Son.

11 And this is the record, that God hath given to us eternal life, and this life is in his Son.

12 He that hath the Son hath life ; *and* he that hath not the Son of God hath not life.

13 These things have I written unto you that believe on the name of the Son of God ; that ye may know that ye have eternal life, and that ye may believe on the name of the Son of God.

REMEMBER that rich young ruler, who, though ardently desiring to possess himself of " eternal life ", yet, because he could not face the condition imposed, forfeited his chance of the gift, and " went away sorrowful, for he had great possessions ", Matthew xix. 22. His earthly possessions, with all their present comfort and prestige, kept him from the eternal possession, which outlives all others, and which outshines them, even here and now. Let it be noted that members of the Fellowship have " great possessions ", of a spiritual sort ; but the first, and last, of them is this greatest of them— " eternal life ", which is the gift that this passage deals with. Which would you rather be, physically—a person with great possessions but no life ; or one with, perhaps, no possessions but life ? Spiritually—we have the greatest of all possessions, which is life itself. You will see that our verses discuss the subject from the point of view, not just of the Gift, but the Giver.

THE WITNESS TO THE REALITY OF THE LIFE-GIVER

John had been one of that devoted company that believed on the Son of GOD. He had gathered with the others for the Master's farewell meeting on Olivet's Mount. He had heard his once crucified, but now living, Lord say, ere the final good-bye—" Ye shall be witnesses unto Me ", Acts i. 8. All his subsequent life he had striven to carry out the Saviour's wish and command. To that end, he had yielded his personality to the HOLY SPIRIT's inspiration for the writing of a Gospel, and a Revelation, and an Epistle. The witness had cost him much, for he had been deported to the rigours of Patmos for the faith, and, if tradition be true, was martyred at the end—thus, like his brother James, years before him, he did " drink indeed of My cup ", Matthew xx. 23, as the Master foretold. At the opening of this Letter he says, concerning the Word of Life, the Lord JESUS, John i. 1, that " the life was manifested, and we have seen it, and bear witness, and shew unto you that eternal life " (i. 2). That has been the main burden of the whole Epistle—which is why the late Mr. George Goodman called his brief study of it *The Epistle of Eternal Life*. And now, as it draws towards its close, the apostle is back again at the theme of the witness.

The Historical Witness—" the witness of men " (9), to JESUS CHRIST. " This is He that came by water and Blood " (6). Says Dr. Vincent, " these words are evidently chosen to describe something characteristic of CHRIST's Messianic office ". Various interpretations of the phrase have been suggested ; but we cannot, for ourselves, avoid coming back to the view that " water and blood " must point to some purely historical facts in the life of our Lord on earth. We recall, then, those three years of His Messianic ministry—at its opening, the Baptism (" by water ") ; at its close, the Crucifixion (" by Blood "). " Not by water only, but by water and Blood "—water only, as if you could dispense with the Blood of His Cross. There are some who preach " a bloodless Gospel ". That omission was the reason why Cain's offering was not acceptable to GOD—there was no blood in it : all which was a figure of things that were to come. Like Cain, some of the extreme modernists imagine that they know better than GOD, and think that salvation can be obtained without the atoning sacrifice. They forget, if they do not despise, the Divine declaration that " without shedding of blood is no remission ", Hebrews ix. 22—either symbolically, as under the Old Dispensation, or actually, as unfolded in the New. How interesting it is that at the completion of the Messianic ministry we are, in symbol, reminded of its opening and finish—" one of the soldiers with a spear pierced His side, and forthwith came there out blood and water ", John xix. 34. " Water "—the sign of the attestation of the well-pleasing Son, Matthew iii. 17, commissioned for His task. " Blood "—the sign of the " finished " accomplishment of the crucified Saviour, John xix. 30, afterwards to be sealed in His resurrection. By the way, have you noticed that in His risen body there is no blood—" a spirit hath not flesh and bones [the usual phrase would be " flesh and blood "] as ye see Me have ", Luke xxiv. 39. His precious Blood had been fully shed for us. There, then, is the historical witness.

Before we pass on, we must deal with that difficult portion in verse 7. You will notice that it is omitted in the Revised Version, and for the following seemingly unanswerable reasons. It is not found in any of the Greek MSS.—except two, one spurious and the other of little weight. It is absent from all the Versions, except the Latin Vulgate, and even from the oldest MSS. of this. It is not mentioned by any of the Greek writers till the thirteenth century, nor any of the Latin authors till the eighth century. This triumvirate of almost complete silence of the old Manuscripts, Versions and Writers, convince us that the verse must be excluded. However, let it be stated, in conclusion, that the words in themselves are not to be taken as untrue, but only as unauthoritative from the viewpoint of Biblical inspiration.

The Spiritual Witness—" the witness of GOD is greater " (9). I think it is true to say that the HOLY SPIRIT has a great passion, which is implied in those words about Him of the Lord JESUS, in John xvi. 14, " He shall glorify Me ". He has done that (a) By writing a Book about Him ; (b) By getting a soul to trust in Him ; (c) By making a Christian to become like to Him ; and adding to this extensive ministry ; (d) By exercising His testimony concerning Him, deigning to confirm " the witness of men "—and whatever may be said of the human frailty of man, this at least will be admitted on all hands that, anyhow, " the SPIRIT is truth " (6). It is the fact, isn't it, that the believer's assurance of salvation is based upon three things—the Work of CHRIST ; the Word of GOD ; and the Witness of the SPIRIT. When anyone rests upon that finished Work, and believes what GOD says about it, then the HOLY SPIRIT brings a conviction to the heart ; so that " he that believeth on the Son of GOD—and the record that GOD gave of His Son—hath the witness in himself " (10). Or, as Paul is led to put it, " The SPIRIT Himself beareth witness with our spirit, that we are the children of GOD ", Romans viii. 16. In passing, don't be confused by that use of the word " Itself " in the Authorised Version into imagining that it lends any support to the idea that the SPIRIT is not a personality. It is only that the *grammatical accuracy* of the Greek calls for it—the word for " Himself " would, of course, be masculine ; but the word for " SPIRIT " is neuter, therefore strictly " Itself ". There is, however, on the *spiritual accuracy* of " Himself ", an abundance of occasions on which that personal pronoun is used—for instance, no less than seven times by our Lord in one verse, John xvi. 13.

So, when we bear witness to our Saviour, either in preaching, or in personal testimony, it is so encouraging to realise that we are doing a work that is of particular interest to the HOLY SPIRIT, and a work to which—either in this case, or in that—He will add His own convincing witness. This is the beginning of, the explanation of, every conversion, or regeneration. The initiative is always with Him. And now mark

THE WORD ABOUT THE RECEPTION OF THE LIFE-GIVER

Here is a Divine Gift—" GOD hath given " (11). Therefore it will have about it all the perfections and excellencies that are associated with the Divine offers to men. And to think that, such is the perversity of the human mind and will, that men and women can be found to refuse the gift. Like the man with the muck-rake, in John Bunyan's *Pilgrim's Progress*, who was so completely concerned with his humble occupation that he had no eyes for the golden crown poised over his head for the taking—that's it with some people, pre-occupation with other, and lesser, things. There are some who fear that to accept the gift would involve them in responsibilities that they cannot face—what others will think, or will say, or will do. Two soldiers—one trying to win his comrade to CHRIST—were talking, when a Christian officer happened to pass, and overheard the unbeliever say, " Well, I just can't face the cost of becoming a Christian ". That fear prevents many from accepting the gift. The officer's retort was note-worthy, " Have you ever faced the cost of *not* becoming a Christian ? " Ah yes, there are many causes (I nearly wrote, reasons !), many excuses, for the strange neglect of GOD'S gift.

Here is a Lasting Gift—" eternal life " (11). So many of our gifts to one another so quickly wear out, or become out-of-fashion ; but here is one that suffers no disability. " For GOD so loved the world that He gave His only begotten Son, that whosoever believeth on Him should . . . have everlasting life ", John iii. 16 : the gift of His life never wears out and is never out-of-fashion. It stands up to all the chances and changes of this mortal realm and is discovered to be all the fashion in the realm above. What a pity—indeed, what a tragedy—that, for the sake of the flimsy and fleeting things of this world, men and women lose this magnificent chance. Says the wise Paul, " We look not at the things which are seen, but at the things which are not seen ; for the things which are seen are temporal, but the things which are not seen are eternal ", II Corinthians iv. 18.

Here is a Personal Gift—(a) " to us " (11). Not just to the mass and multitude of men, but to me personally, and to you : to all of us, but to each of us. Listen to Paul again, who, as we should expect, so often corroborates the teaching of the beloved John, for it is the same SPIRIT Who inspires them both—" the life which I now live, I live by the faith on the Son of GOD, Who loved *me*, and gave Himself for *me* ", Galatians ii. 20. There is not a soul, not even the worst and wickedest, that He doesn't love, and that cannot have the gift, on the twin conditions of repentance and faith—so per-sonal is the gift. But it is that also in another sense. (b) " This life is in His Son " (11). It is not so much it, as He. How often have we blessed GOD that the Master *is* what He *gives*. " I am the Door "—not merely opens it, but is it. The Entrance " in " to salvation, and " out " for service, John x. 9. " I am the Way "—not just shows it, but is it. The true and the living Way, John xiv. 6. " I am that Bread " —not simply gives it, but is it. The sustaining, satisfying

Bread that is ever new, John vi. 48. So, " I am the Resurrection and the Life "—not only has it, but is it. The life that is life indeed, John xi. 25. Thus our passage presses home to our hearts the vital truth, " He that hath the Son hath [the] life " (12)—not just life in the ordinary, physical sense, but " the life ", and the definite article is in the Greek, the life that he has all along been talking about, the life that is of that eternally enduring quality, that life which becomes ours as soon as He becomes ours—gift to a person, of a Person, by a Person.

Here is a Certain Gift—" ye may know that ye have " (13). That, says this author, is the reason why he has written as he has—in order that the believers he writes to may be quite sure that they have this priceless possession of eternal life, because they have the Life-giver. There are those who say that you can't know until you get there ; but this Scripture says, " ye may know ". There are others who say that it is presumption to talk like this ; but our verse says, " that ye have ". We ask which is the more presumptuous—to believe GOD's word, or to doubt it ? John and Paul are full of sublime certitudes, because they base their certainty, not on their own merit, or power, but only on the wondrous mercy and grace of the Almighty GOD. C. H. Spurgeon, when preaching on John v. 24, " hath everlasting life ", exclaimed, shutting his fist up tight as he pronounced the word—" H-A-T-H spells GOT IT ". Peculiar spelling, but glorious truth. Don't pass by the thought in our verse that the assurance is given to " you that believe on the Name of the Son of GOD "—the title is the pledge of the confidence ; the Name is the surety for our sureness.

Do you notice the strange repetition of words in that 13th verse—" These things have I written unto you that believe on the Name of the Son of GOD . . . that ye may believe on the Name of the Son of GOD ". Do they not lend support to the thesis that we propounded in our last study, that faith is the principle of the Christian life—not only in its beginning, but in its continuing all through. You do believe : very well, then you are to go on believing—and you have a sure foundation to begin with, that your receiving hand of faith has gotten the Gift. Not that you *think* you have, nor *hope* you have, nor *feel* you have, but that you *know* you have. GOD says it, and I believe it.

Here is an Omnibus Gift—I am reminded that, at one Christmas, I was given a present of a compactum. It was a delightful box, well made, and nice to look at. Yes ; but inside were many little compartments, stocked with all sorts of useful things—pins, paper-fasteners, indiarubber, luggage labels, sticking-paper, and so on. Well now, in GOD's preeminent gift of Eternal Life, there are contained so many blessings, for the meeting of so many needs—they are all there " in CHRIST ", Who is Himself the Life. Our grateful thoughts go back to the wondrous words of Romans viii. 32, " He that spared not His own Son, but delivered Him up for us all, how shall He not with Him also freely give us all things ? " All the gifts are in the Gift of the Life-giver.

THE WARNING CONCERNING THE REJECTION OF THE LIFE-GIVER

" He that hath not the Son of GOD hath not life " (13). That solemn statement embraces two consequential issues—a positive and a negative, each of which is charged, for this unbeliever, with enormous significance. And we recall that to neglect is the equivalent of to reject—" How shall we escape if we *neglect* so great salvation ? ", Hebrews ii. 3. In this eternally decisive matter, to say nothing is to say " No ".

The Positive Consequence—of such an attitude is the dread sentence of the " second death ", Revelation xx. 14. We shall say nothing here in explanation of it. Far better to leave the matter to the actual words of Holy Scripture. Whatever our opinion may be, there it is : the alternative to such a Life is such a Death. Let us stay only to remark that we may rest assured that no one will suffer that penalty without every chance to " escape "—for GOD, in His love and mercy, has made " a way to escape ", I Corinthians x. 13, by the way of the Cross. We may be sure, further, that nothing in this will impugn, or controvert, God's impeccable justice.

The Negative Consequence—of this negative response is the loss of all the delights, the blessings, the powers, the service, wrapped up in this omnibus gift. Pardon of sins, peace of mind, prosperity of spirit, pleasure of heart, power for service, prayer for others, possibility of His likeness, prospect of glory —" in CHRIST ", all are ours ; apart from Him, nothing is ours.

What a possession, then, is this Life in the Life-giver—a life that *Grows*, II Peter iii. 18 ; that *Knows*, I John ii. 20 ; that *Shows*, Luke viii. 39 ; that *Flows*, John vii. 38 ; that *Glows*, Psalm xxxiv. 5, American R.V., " radiant '

May all Fellowship members " possess their possessions ", Obadiah 17.

XIII

THE PRAYERS OF THE FELLOWSHIP

I JOHN v. 14-17

14 And this is the confidence that we have in him, that, if we ask any thing according to his will, he heareth us :

15 And if we know that he hear us, whatsoever we ask, we know that we have the petitions that we desired of him.

16 If any man see his brother sin a sin *which is* not unto death, he shall ask, and he shall give him life for them that sin not unto death. There is a sin unto death : I do not say that he shall pray for it.

17 All unrighteousness is sin : and there is a sin not unto death.

THE Epistle is hurrying to its close. There have been occasions while he has been writing when, looking back upon what has already been said, John tackles again subjects already dealt with, enlarging the treatment of the matter or underlining it for the sake of stressing its importance. That is what happens in these verses. He has already spoken of the supreme ministry of prayer ; and now, that the members of the Fellowship shall realise to the full the power and the privilege of it, he takes it in hand once more.

ITS TWOFOLD EFFECT

There are those who would say that it has no effect at all. Yet that was not what Moses found, nor David found, nor Elijah found, nor Daniel found, nor Nehemiah found, nor Paul found, nor Epaphras found, nor the church found, nor—may I add—what CHRIST found. All these, and many others then and since, down through the years testify to the intrinsic worth, and immense work, of prayer. " This is the confidence that we have in Him " (14), would be the common testimony of a myriad saints. What, then, does prayer do ?

Its subjective effect—in our own heart and being, keeping us fresh, according to Isaiah xl. 31, " They that wait upon the LORD shall renew their strength ; they shall mount up with wings as eagles, they shall run and not be weary, they shall

walk and not faint ". The mountain-top breezes of prayer,
so dear to the heart of our Lord, Who so often " went up into
a mountain apart to pray ", Matthew xiv. 23—how invigorat-
ing they are. The open windows of prayer, as practiced by
the intrepid warrior, who " his windows being open . . . he
kneeled upon his knees . . . and prayed ", Daniel vi. 10—
how symbolic of the freshening of spirit brought by this exercise of the soul. Freshness, yes ; and strength, too, does
prayer bring to our hearts. Archbishop Trench's words are
so true still—

> " We kneel, how weak ; we rise, how full of strength,
> Why, therefore, do we do ourselves this wrong,
> And others—that we are not always strong ? "

If this were all that prayer does, how well worthwhile it
would be ; but it is not all.

Its objective effect—it obtains things from GOD ; it gets
things done. Indeed, it is no exaggeration to say that it is
the chief instrument for getting GOD's will done on earth.
Oh, says some unbeliever—who, incidentally, has never prayed
properly, and so knows nothing about the matter—this
universe has been so constituted by Nature (as he puts it)
as to be governed by Law, and your prayer cannot alter that.
Laws : how true—and all the various laws subserve each
other, work in with each other : the law of magnetism counter-
acting the law of gravity, for instance. Laws : how true—
and the law of prayer is one of them. The incontrovertible
experience of the saints is, that GOD does things because of
prayer that he does not do without it. What is the use of
the objector saying that prayer accomplishes nothing, in the
face of the work of George Müller and his great Orphanage.
Beginning in a small way, it grew to great proportions—so that
during the space of something like sixty years, he clothed, fed,
educated, and cared for some thousands of children, and
gathered in nearly two million pounds for the doing of it.
He made it his rule never to advertise, nor to ask anyone
for a penny ; but simply to tell GOD, and ask Him for all
supplies. He and his workers adhered to that rule through
all that long period—and all their needs were supplied,
whether in the day-by-day necessities, or in the matter of
bigger demands. Simply and solely by prayer. Talk about

" pennies from heaven "—pounds, too! Now that is a
dramatic example of the workings of the Law of Prayer.
How many stories could be told of GOD's answers to prayer—
for Provision, for Guidance, for Strength, for Protection, oh,
and what not. Even, at times, about the weather, James
v. 17-18.

It is this objective side of the matter that is the theme of
this passage—as is evidenced by the word employed, " we
know that we have the *petitions* that we desired of Him "
(15). And here again, as he deals with the subject, John does
not fail to indicate that the " any thing " of our verse 14, like
the " whatsoever " of iii. 22, is dependent upon conditions.
Putting the two passages, indeed the whole Epistle, together,
we may say that the governing factors of successful prayer
are—*Being*: that is, " born of GOD ". *Obeying*: " because
we keep His commandments ". *Dwelling*: " we dwell in
Him, and He in us ". *Knowing*: " according to His will ".
Then, simply, *Asking*: for the definite thing. So comes the
Receiving: " we have the petitions ". Westcott says that
" the believer would not make his own any prayer which is
not according to GOD's will. And since he has made GOD's
will his own will, he has all he truly seeks in immediate and
present possession. [Note Mark xi. 24, ' What things soever
ye desire, when ye pray, believe that ye receive them, and
ye shall have them '.], though the visible fulfilment may be
delayed ". That is, as it seems to me, a very profound statement. Yes, if we ask, He will do. Here is another amazing
potentiality belonging to the members of the Fellowship.
Now look at something else.

ITS TWOFOLD ASPECT

Two different words are used here, to describe different
kinds of prayer. The distinction is not unimportant ; and
any point that leads us to a wider and deeper understanding
of this mighty ministry is infinitely worth-while, isn't it ?
Some of us Christians are content with just " saying our
prayers " every morning and night, a habit which can be full
of earnest reality, but which also can degenerate into a mere
formality. How marked an influence we could exert upon
our friends and neighbours, and right across the world in
distant lands, if we were to engage in a ministry of unhurried

intercession, at some regularly adopted period of the day or week—getting alone with GOD in the quiet, perhaps with a map of the world before you, perhaps with a street directory of your own district ; and thus go from place to place, and pray. Who can measure what might be accomplished in this way. It was thus that an invalid lady brought D. L. Moody to Great Britain. Listen afresh to your Master, " When thou prayest, enter into thy closet, and when thou hast shut thy door, pray to thy Father which is in secret ; and thy Father . . . shall reward thee openly ", Matthew vi. 6. We spoke just now of the Open Window of prayer ; here it is the Shut Door ! Well, what about those two words we mentioned ? They are both here in the passage before us.

The Ordinary Word—is the one that is most often used for prayer. It is the one that is, in this passage, translated " ask ". It is used in the familiar passage of Matthew vii. 7, " Ask, and it shall be given you ", and in many other places. One might almost call it the subordinate's word. It represents the plea of an inferior to a superior, a pupil to a master, a servant to an employer, a subject to a king, and so of a man to GOD. When we come to GOD in prayer, we must always remember that we are speaking to the All-mighty, the All-holy, the All-highest—anything other than uttermost reverence is altogether unbecoming in the suppliants at the Divine throne. Except for one thing, it would be impossible for man to approach GOD at all. That one thing is, that GOD Himself has taken the initiative—He has opened the way, He has granted the audience. And so, for our encouragement, we read, " Having therefore, brethren, boldness to enter into the holiest by the Blood of JESUS ", Hebrews x. 19, the ground of access. And, " Let us, therefore, come boldly unto the throne of grace, that we may obtain mercy, and find grace to help in time of need ", Hebrews iv. 16, the use of access. Thus, in all humble dependence, yet in bright hope, because He has bidden us come, and " ask ", we members of the Fellowship can gladly exercise our privilege, and intercede.

The Out-of-the-Ordinary Word—now calls for our attention. It is used in our passage but once, and is there translated, " pray " (16). This word is used of the requests of an equal to an equal ; and is the one employed when speaking of the Lord's praying to His Father. That first word, of the inferior, is never adopted concerning His approach to GOD. The study of the use of words in Scripture is most fascinating ; and it confirms me in the old belief in the Divine verbal inspiration of the Bible, as originally given—not the Authorised Version, please, much as I love it, nor the Moffatt Paraphrase ; but as first written.

Now, the amazing thing is that GOD allows some people, sometimes, to speak to Him in this more intimate way— almost on an equal footing. He has no favourites, but He has intimates—shall we put it, those who have an absorbing love for Him, for any other condition is wrapped up in that. Such people have an entrée to the presence and ear of GOD that is peculiarly near ; and while normally, like the rest of us, they " ask " in the ordinary way, there are occasions, times, subjects, in which they may " pray " in the closer fashion, as friend with Friend, John xv. 14, as beloved son with Father. Take a prince of the Royal House—he will make his requests to his father in a twofold manner. Some-times as to the King, when he will " ask ", as the inferior subject of his Sovereign ; but sometimes, in the privacy of the family, he will " pray " him, on equal terms, as the son of his Sire—but always with the respect due to the exalted station of the monarch. It is a faint picture of the dual prayer relationship that our GOD has graciously allowed His intimates. It naturally follows that the inner prayer can seek for further things, deeper things, greater things, than the ordinary prayer —do you not think that George Müller's intercession was in this holy category ? But—there is sometimes a limit even to this kind. Why did Abraham cease in his intercession as he did ? Because he had reached the limit—GOD terminated the interview, " the LORD went His way ", Genesis xviii. 33. No, Abraham, you must not pray for Sodom to be spared. Here is the same principle in our passage. Whatever be the nature of this sin, GOD declares through John, " I do not say that he shall *pray* for it " (16). No, not even that special, intimate prayer shall seek for that. One is reminded of that sore judgment, " Ephraim is joined to idols : let him alone " (Hosea iv. 17). Let him alone ! " I do not say that he shall pray for it." Thank GOD, Ephraim's backsliding was eventu-ally " healed " (xiv. 4), because " Ephraim shall say, What have I to do any more with idols " (xiv. 8). The sin must take its course, " let him alone "—until his repentance, and

GOD's mercy, shall coincide for eventual blessing. **Oh, how
GOD hates the sin, oh, how GOD loves the sinner! And now**
note concerning prayer.

ITS TWOFOLD OBJECT

For Ourselves. It is reassuring to know that we may " ask
anything " (14). It may be a very foolish thing; but GOD
is able to sort things out, and if that request be not good,
He will, in His answer, give something ministering to our
well-being. He saw it was foolish of Paul to seek riddance of
his " thorn in the flesh ", so He gave him instead grace to
bear it, II Corinthians xii. 7–9. It may be a very material
thing; but GOD is interested in our material welfare. Yes,
" anything ". He will not chide us for our wrongful asking,
but, moulding His provision to the shape of our request, will
grant us as is " according to His will ".

So may we " ask " in " confidence "—not in our eloquence,
not in our fervency, not in our merit, or desert; but " that
we have in Him ". He has undertaken to listen, He has
promised to answer; and we confidently rely on His word.
" We know that we have the petitions that we desired of
Him " (15)—provided they were His will for us. We turn
to consider the other object of our prayers—

For Others. The proper description of the previous kind of
prayer is Petition, while this is Intercession. The passage
does not roam at large, but deals with a specific matter concerning the spiritual life of others. Note, further, that the
verses do not deal with prayer for the unconverted just now,
though they are not to be excluded from the influence of this
ministry. You will remember that in the Lord's Prayer we
have the same momentary omission, " I pray not for the
world ", John xvii. 9—he means, not just at the moment.
For those outside the Kingdom, we are entitled, encouraged,
and enabled to pray. Some of them will not let you talk to
them about GOD; but they cannot prevent you talking to
GOD about them. One day He may rejoice your heart by
giving you the chance to answer your own prayer, and present
you with the GOD-made opportunity to lead them to Himself.

But it is the " brother " that is here in mind—which means
that He is a member of the same Family, a child of the same
Father, as yourself, a fellow member of the Fellowship

What, then, is this " sin unto death " ?   A number of sugges-
tions have been advanced ; and I should think it is well not
to be too dogmatic ; but what I have said under the " Out-
of-the-ordinary word " will indicate what is my own view of
the matter. Only I would stress that it is my opinion only,
for anything that it may be worth.   I think, then, that the
" death " is physical death.

What is known as the Unpardonable Sin is a specific transgression, which, as Matthew xii. 31–2 makes clear, is the
persistent rejection of the testimony of the HOLY SPIRIT concerning the Lord JESUS ; but I take it that this Sin unto
Death is not any one particular wrong, and the " a " (16)
would be best omitted as, of course, the Greek would allow—
that is, there is such a thing as sin that might lead to death.
We know that it has led to spiritual death—" in the day that
thou eatest thereof thou shalt surely die ", Genesis ii. 17—
and he did die, spiritually, that moment, and all his entail
following.   " As by one man sin entered into the world, and
death by sin ; and so death passed upon all men, for that all
have sinned ", Romans v. 12.   If, when John said, " there is
sin not unto death " (17), it would be a complete contradiction of this fundamental passage, if he had meant spiritual
death.   But, as it appears to me, physical death puts the
matter straight, and there is no contradiction.   When a
Christian falls to sinning, his salvation is not jeopardised, he
does not revert to his unregenerate state of spiritual death ;
but, in certain cases, he may incur the penalty of physical
death.   The Christians at Corinth were the victims of this
sore displeasure of the Lord, because in some flagrant way
they had abused the Lord's Supper—" for this cause many
are weak and sickly among you, and many sleep ", I Corinthians xi. 30.   The physical death of the believer is described
by our Lord as " sleep ", Mark v. 39 ; John xi. 11–13. Spiritual death is never associated with a believer, because, says
the Lord, with all the added weight of His doubly emphatic,
" Verily, verily ", he " is passed from death unto life ", John
v. 24.   It is, then, a physical chastening of the Lord that is,
in our belief, spoken of here, whether of sickness, or in extreme
cases, of death ; and, as the Corinthian passage continues,
in verse 32, " we are chastened of the Lord, that we should
not be condemned with the world ".   Somewhat in this sense,
says Dr. Pettingill, of America, Moses sinned unto death,

Deuteronomy xxxii. 48–52 ; Achan sinned unto death, Joshua vii. 25 ; Ananias sinned unto death, Acts v. 1–11.

This, then, whatever be its true meaning, is the one forbidden ground. How vast, however, is the area of permissive prayer, wherein the Fellowship can exercise this ministry for the " brother ", or for the other. To return to our previous image let us to such purpose open our windows of prayer that GOD will " open you the windows of heaven, and pour you out a blessing that there shall not be room enough to receive it ", Malachi iii. 10—all you can do with such abundance is to overflow it to others ; even " rivers of living water ", John vii. 38.

XIV

THE PERSUASIONS OF THE FELLOWSHIP

I JOHN v. 18–21

18 We know that whosoever is born of God sinneth not; but he that is begotten of God keepeth himself, and that wicked one toucheth him not.

19 *And* we know that we are of God, and the whole world lieth in wickedness.

20 And we know that the Son of God is come, and hath given us an understanding, that we may know him that is true, and we are in him that is true, *even* in his Son Jesus Christ. This is the true God, and eternal life.

21 Little children, keep yourselves from idols. Amen.

"WE know . . ." (18); "And we know . . ." (19); "And we know . . ." (20). This is a characteristic word of the apostle's—seven times over it comes within the brief space of verses 13–20 of this chapter. Indeed, he states that, as we have already remarked, while he wrote the Gospel that "ye might *have* life", John xx. 31, he penned the Epistle "that ye may *know* that ye have eternal life", I John v. 13. You see, there are certain fundamental things about which, like Paul, we may say, "I am persuaded . . .", Romans viii. 38. We need not be afraid, nor ashamed, of such blessed dogmatism, when it is based, not on our opinion, but on the specific Word of GOD.

Let the believer, then, rest his case, take his stand, upon such rock-like foundations, amid all the winds that blow, and the waves that threaten. In the world in which he is situate, he will experience much opposition, and many perplexities; theories and problems will engage his attention, and sometimes even question his Christian belief. There is a fundamental principle which should always keep him steady: Don't let what you know be upset by what you don't know. Resting upon "Thus saith the Lord", he need not quail before what saith the world. Take as example the testimony of an erstwhile blind man, in answer to the quibbling assertions of unbelievers—"Whether he be a sinner or no, I know not:

one thing I know, that whereas I was blind, now I see ",
John ix. 25. Come with me, then, as we close our meditations
on this wonderful Epistle, and let us study together these
three great certitudes, with which our inspired author con-
cludes—three that he is led to select here out of many ; three
that should make for the establishment in faith and life of
every true member of the Fellowship.

Concerning Christian Purity

" We know . . ." (18). How careful the Epistle has been all
through to insist that the Christian life is a holy life, thus
marking out the teaching of Christianity as something wholly
different from that of other religions. In the eyes of the New
Testament, an unholy Christian is an anomaly, a contradiction
in terms—an unsaintly saint : no, no ! Yet, alas, such a
monstrosity is not uncommon. Had we better look into our
own hearts, do you think ?

The Fact Stated. (*a*) " Whosoever is born of GOD ", not
the well-meaning, not the hard-trier, not the new-leafer, but
the really regenerate, the new " I " of Galatians ii. 20. Of
such an one, here is a remarkable statement. (*b*) " Sinneth
not "—a present tense, denoting not an isolated, or occasional
wrongdoing, but a continual course of sin. Alas, we Christians
do sometimes fall, though we need not ; but this is a very
different thing. In the old days, he travelled through life
" according to the course of this world, according to the
prince of the power of the air, the spirit that now worketh in
the children of disobedience ", Ephesians ii. 2. But, by the
grace of GOD, and by the new birth of the SPIRIT, the believer
has now changed his course. He may sometimes go wrong ;
but he won't go on in it.

The Fact Emphasised—" that wicked one toucheth him
not ". The word is stronger than the Authorised Version
represents—nearer to the idea of the original would be, " lays
no hold on him ". You have the same word in the Lord's
" Touch Me not ", in John xx. 17, where it is again the laying
hold that He forbids, as if Mary, in symbol, would seek to
detain Him here, and deter His departure back to Heaven.
When He has " ascended ", she may lay hold of Him in
spirit ; but meanwhile she must not clasp Him in body—
the old physical relationship no longer obtains. So, then, let

the believer rejoice that, though the wicked one may lay a hand on him, to try to turn him aside, yet he can never lay hold on him, to compel him thither. Let it not be forgotten that the devil cannot *make* us sin.

The Fact Explained—" he that is begotten of GOD keepeth himself ". When we were considering the phrase " Him that is begotten of Him " (1) we had the great authority of Westcott for saying that the whole context indicated that the begotten one was the believer, the son of GOD—" the child who draws from Him the abiding principle of his life ". Now, in our present verse, we have the great weight of the same scholar for holding that the context in this case demands that " He that is begotten of GOD " refers, not to the son of GOD, but to the Son of GOD. There follows from that a great change in the verse. It is not to remain " keepeth himself ", but " keepeth him ". He does not depend on his own strength or vigilance. He has an active Enemy, but he has also a watchful Guardian. The glorious certainty of the Christian's daily victory and purity rests on the sublime fact that the " only begotten Son ", Whom GOD " gave ", John iii. 16, and " sent ", I John iv. 10, keeps him safe. The One Who is " able to save to the uttermost ", Hebrews vii. 25, is also " able to keep you from falling ", Jude 24. When the little child takes hold of the policeman's hand, he takes hold of hers ; and her safety in crossing that busy street lies, not in her hold, though that had to be there, but in his. Thus it is that the Psalmist is able confidently to say, " Hold Thou me up, and I shall be safe ", Psalm cxix. 117. And that is why it is no presumption to say about the glorious possibility of purity, " We know . . .".

Concerning Christian Position

" We know . . ." (19). We have, under the guidance of our writer, devoted a whole study to the consideration of this theme, and now, because of its importance for all Christian health and happiness, the apostle calls us back again to it, that we may be perfectly sure where we live—the soul's house into which we enter, for all that salvation stands for ; from which we emerge, for all the service that salvation leads to. John underlines then—

The Certainty of the Believer's Situation. We are " of GOD ".

We are in the Family, in the Fellowship with all that that means, as revealed in the Epistle—with a Forgiven Past, and a Fearless Present, and a Fine Prospect. We "know" this: whatever other people may say, whatever we may sometimes feel, whatever opposition we may encounter. Again we say that it is no presumption to avow this in such certain tones, for it is founded, not on our being better than others, but on our believing GOD—the "better" should come afterwards. I say "should", because, alas, it does not always do so. It is the sad fact that, in not a few instances, men and women of the world often put us Christians to shame, in the uprightness of their character, in the kindliness of their disposition, and in the helpfulness of their behaviour—not always, by any means, but sometimes. The Christian should always be a better man than the worldling; but, better or not, he is different. His situation is different, as John here sums it up, in recalling the phrase, "we are in Him" (20)—oh, blessed privilege, protection, potentiality, purpose, and provision. "In Him"! Look at the situation as it is typified in the experience of Moses, "Behold, there is a place by Me, and thou shalt stand upon a rock, and . . . I will put thee in a clift of the rock, and will cover thee with My hand", Exodus xxxiii. 21–22. On the rock, in the rock—even the Rock of Ages cleft for me! All that, and much more that only glory will reveal, because of our situation, "of GOD". We know that!

The Contrast of the Unbeliever's Situation. "The whole world lieth in wickedness". Or, rather, in the Wicked One. In ii. 20, we have a comparable phrase, "the Holy One"; and it would appear that, as in physical geography, so in the geography of the spirit, there are two hemispheres—and, according to his relationship to CHRIST, every person has his situation clearly defined: he dwells either in the Holy One, or in the Wicked One. All the worldlings are positioned in the latter. The devil, says our Lord, is "the prince of this world", who has usurped the Saviour's lawful throne, who is already "judged", John xvi. 11, who shall be "cast out", John xii. 31, and who hath "nothing in Me", John xiv. 30. He is, says Paul, "the god of this world", II Corinthians iv. 4, who has blinded the eyes of the unbeliever—so that, on the one hand, he cannot see the beauties and glories of CHRIST, and, on the other hand, cannot see the losses and perils of his situation.

Thank GOD, it is possible to emigrate from this barren hemisphere of darkness to the joyous region of light. He, Whom this very writer has recorded as saying " I am the Way ", John xiv. 6, invites us to put our hand of faith in His, and He will tightly grasp, and firmly hold, and safely land us in the glad hemisphere, where reign eternal life, and light, and love. Members of the Fellowship " know " that, by the grace and mercy of GOD, they dwell there ; and if their membership is the virile reality that it is expected to be, they will be eager to stretch out the hands of their loving service, to fetch others in.

> " O strengthen me, that while I stand
> Firm on the rock, and strong in Thee,
> I may stretch out a loving hand
> To wrestlers in life's troubled sea."

CONCERNING CHRISTIAN PERCEPTION

" We know . . ." (20). Members of the Fellowship, by reason of their new birth, have come to a new understanding of things. Take the story of Naaman's cleansing as typical of our cleansing from the leprosy of sin, and mark how the miracle of mercy brings him into a different view of things. " Behold, I thought . . .", II Kings v. 11. Wrong plan—as if his cleansing (or ours) could be bought. Wrong person—as if the king (or, with us, anyone but JESUS) could do it. Wrong place—as if other rivers than Jordan (picture, for us, of the stream that flows from Calvary's mountain) could effect it. Wrong power—as if some energy of the flesh (instead of, in our case, trust in the Divine energy) were required. He was all wrong, as so many unregenerate people are. " Behold, now I know . . ." (15)—that there is but One GOD Who can cleanse and save. After his new birth, if you like—for " his flesh came again, like unto the flesh of a little child " (14)— he knew so differently. It is a vivid picture of the new understanding that comes to the one who has become a member of the Family, the Fellowship. " The natural man ", the unregenerate man, just can't see, and will not accept it, I Corinthians ii. 14. But thank GOD for " the eyes of your understanding being enlightened ", Ephesians i. 18.

The Source of it—(a) " the Son of GOD is come "—not only into the world, but into our hearts. If He had not, we had nothing. (b) "and hath given us an understanding "—a grasp of holy things that will never accrue to us by any human reasoning. But " GOD hath revealed them unto us by His SPIRIT ", I Corinthians ii. 10. As we saw in ii. 20, " ye have an unction from the Holy One, and ye know all things "—that is, are in a position to get to know all things that are needful for your spiritual growth and well-being.

The Object of it—" that we may know Him that is true ". As we come to know more and more of His ways among men, and of His will for men, so we shall see more and more of His Divine nature, and so we shall come to love Him more and more deeply, as the days go by. There is an ever deepening knowledge of Him, that every earnest member of the Fellowship will assuredly covet. Paul came first to know Him on the Damascus road, when, in response to his mystified " Who art Thou . . . ? ", came the revelation that He was the Living Lord JESUS. From that moment of destiny he knew Him; but listen to him, as he writes years afterwards, " That I may know Him ", Philippians iii. 10.

The Secret of it—" we are in Him that is true ". As we said earlier, you never really know a person until you live with him. And here it is again, that because we are " in Him ", we can increasingly know Him and understand His mind and will. By the way, you will have observed how often in our study I have repeated myself—that is only because the Epistle itself does the same. John desires, by this method of the true teacher, to instruct by repetition—to say it again, to stress the importance of the matter, and to impress the mind and memory of his readers with the truth concerned. So he has laid lasting emphasis upon the full Deity of JESUS CHRIST— " true GOD "; and upon the all-embracing boon that He is to us—" eternal life ".

The Responsibility of it—" little children, keep yourselves from idols " (21). We have just learned that we cannot keep ourselves; but the word for " keep " here is a different one. In the present sense, we are enjoined to do it. An idol is, of course, anyone, or anything, that takes the place that GOD should have in our lives. Mr. R. M. L. Waugh, in his recently published book, *The Preacher and His Greek Testament*, reminds us that " We live in an age of god-makers. Narcissus, god of Self [fell in love with his own reflection in a pool]. Mars, god of War. Bacchus, god of Wine. Venus, goddess of Love. Apollo, god of physical Beauty. Minerva, goddess of Science. Fortuna, goddess of Luck. Golden Calf, god of Money." It is for us to keep any such unworthy displacement away. Fellowship members have been given a perception, an understanding, that is denied to others. They surely should know the supreme worthiness of GOD, on the one hand, and the comparative worthlessness of idols, on the other hand, sufficiently to ensure that they " keep themselves from idols ". The word here translated " keep " should be " guard ".

So, we " little children " have learnt herein—what we ought to be, what we ought to do, what we ought to know, because we are members of the Fellowship.

The other day I came across these lines, wherein, as in soliloquy, Anna Barbauld speaks of her parting with life here and taking it up again hereafter—

> " Life ! we've been long together,
> Through pleasant and through cloudy weather ;
> 'Tis hard to part when friends are dear—
> Perhaps 'twill cost a sigh, a tear ;
> —Then steal away, give little warning,
> Choose thine own time ;
> Say not Good night—but in some brighter clime
> Bid me Good morning."

Ay, all ye Fellowship Members, we'll meet in the Morning !